Stepping Stones
to Science

Stepping Stones to Science

True Tales and Awesome Activities

KENDALL HAVEN

1997
TEACHER IDEAS PRESS
A Division of
Libraries Unlimited, Inc.
Englewood, Colorado

This book is dedicated to curiosity, wonder, imagination, and perseverance—the four cornerstones of good science and good stories.

■

TEACHER IDEAS PRESS
A Division of
Libraries Unlimited, Inc.
P.O. Box 6633
Englewood, CO 80155-6633
1-800-237-6124
www.lu.com/tip

Production Editor: Kevin W. Perizzolo
Copy Editor: D. Aviva Rothschild
Proofreader: Susie Sigman
Indexer: Nancy Fulton
Typesetter: Kay Minnis

Library of Congress Cataloging-in-Publication Data

Haven, Kendall F.
    Stepping stones to science : true tales and awesome activities / by Kendall Haven.
        xi, 155 p. 22x28 cm.
        Includes bibliographical references and index.
        ISBN 1-56308-516-X
        1. Science--Study and teaching. 2. Science--Methodology--Study and teaching. 3. Science--Experiments. 4. Discoveries in science.
    I. Title.
Q181.H3755   1997
372.3'5044--DC21   97-7629
                                                                                   CIP

Contents

Physics

Electricity

Chemistry

BIOLOGICAL SCIENCES

Introduction

"Tell me a story!" Children learn these magic words almost as soon as they learn to speak. The phrase is always said with an eager smile, security blanket tucked under one arm, thumb comfortably slipped into the mouth. "Tell me a story!" Witches, goblins, wizards, heroes, monsters, enchanted keys—it seems any story will do.

Then we begin to teach, and we tend to separate the enchantment of story from the rigors of core curriculum instruction. But stories are all about teaching and learning. Learning is all about stories. I have worked with hundreds of teachers across the country who have come to see that stories are a more effective and efficient way to teach both factual and conceptual information. High school students, sixth graders, college seniors, kindergartners . . . they can all benefit from and learn through stories.

When I say "story," many really hear "made-up story" or at least "fictional story." Fiction stories are certainly exciting and engrossing. However, so are real-life stories from all aspects of our shared history. I have come to believe that of all the historical fields, disciplines, and subjects, science stories are the best of all. Science is stuffed with more than enough risk, drama, intrigue, courage, mystery, struggle, brashness, daring, greed, deceit, and boldness to support a juicy soap opera for years. Science is loaded with great stories!

I didn't always think so. As a child I thought science was as boring as everyone else did. Not only did I believe that *studying* science was boring, I assumed that *doing* science must be equally boring. When I was in junior high, I remember thinking that Isaac Newton must have awakened one day itching with restlessness, weighed down by boredom. He stretched and muttered, "Ho, hum. It's been a while since I was in the spotlight. Guess I'll invent gravity today and be a celebrity." He got dressed and wandered outside looking for something symbolic. And bam! There dangled a conveniently poised apple just waiting for an opportune moment to fall.

Wrong! It didn't happen that way at all. Newton was tormented for years by nagging questions. Apples fell. Rocks fell. Even rain fell. What made them fall? Why didn't the Moon also fall? Why didn't the stars fall? Why didn't the Earth fall into the Sun? What made small things fall but ignored large things (moons, stars, and planets)?

When the apple fell, it gave him no answers. He didn't sit up and say, "Aha! Gravity!" The falling apple helped him formulate his question in a more useful way. Thus, when he received new information (in the form of a young nephew spinning a ball on the end of a string), he was better prepared to recognize his answer.

And what a glorious moment when the answer came! The grand epiphany as long-sought understanding flooded into his mind. Few of us ever get moments of such all-consuming excitement and triumph. But science is stuffed with thousands of such moments: large moments that shake the Earth and human beliefs, smaller moments of personal insight and victory. They all make wonderful stories.

Thirteen such moments appear in this book. They come from physical, biological, and earth sciences. They each link well with the primary science curriculum. I chose these stories because I find each one to be a fascinating tale. More important, they each demonstrate the "doing" of science. That is, they each present a preeminent scientist following the precepts of the scientific method of investigation. These stories show both the content and process of science.

You will not learn theorems, equations, or formulas in these stories. Instead, you and your students will taste the exciting roller-coaster ride of science, the wonder of pushing into the unknown, the thrill of discovery. You will gain an appreciation for the demands of the process, the journey of doing science, and the vast variety of personalities who have graced that world.

I owe a great debt of thanks and appreciation to eight individuals whose insightful council have done much to shape this book.

Dr. Nelson Kellogg is the only person I have ever heard of, or met, with a doctorate in the history of science. He has been an inexhaustible fountain of ideas, insights, and inspiration.

Six primary grade teachers critiqued each of these stories and generously provided valuable content and format ideas. My unending thanks go out to Cecilia Dearborn and Cheryl Pennington of California, Roberta Schram of Maryland, Carolyn Truseman of Idaho, Robert Frankel of Florida, and Pam Gooden of South Carolina.

My greatest thanks and appreciation go to Roni Berg, an intelligent, insightful woman who finds science exceedingly dull. She was my litmus test for each story, and helped make each story interesting, readable, and understandable. For that help I am eternally grateful.

Lastly, I want to encourage each of you to do more than just read these stories and use the follow-up activities. This book includes only a baker's dozen of stories. There are thousands waiting to be discovered and told. Find them. Tell them. Share them. We will all be better off.

I hope you find the science and scientists inhabiting these pages to be more interesting and exciting than you ever thought they could be.

How to Use This Book

In addition to the actual story test, each story in this book includes a variety of pre-story and post-story sections to focus and heighten student enjoyment, understanding, and learning from the stories. These additional elements are included to assist the integration of the stories into science curriculum teaching. A brief word about the intended use of each element is in order.

1. Pre-Story Elements.

    A Point to Ponder. Allow a few minutes for class discussion on these open-ended questions before diving into the story. They have been written to focus student interest and attention on the story's central science themes, and to move their thinking more in line with the thoughts and dilemmas of the central characters.

    Science Curriculum Links. These stories are closely linked with key aspects of the science framework for most states. These paragraphs are included to assist teachers in better placing the stories within the overall flow of their science teaching.

    Key Picture-Maker Words. Stories revolve around vivid images. Images come from nouns. However, some key nouns in the stories may be unfamiliar to some primary students. To the extent that I could anticipate them, I have included unfamiliar, unclear words and concepts in this section. Each listing includes both a brief definition and guidance on ways to make the concept vivid and clear before launching into the story.

2. Post-Story Elements.

    Topics to Talk About. Stories are about specific characters and specific events. Teachers will find it valuable to review those specifics following a story and to explain them in more general terms, connecting them to the lives of the students. This section includes suggested follow-up discussion topics and guided questions and answers to relate the story to core science concepts and themes and to students' daily experiences.

    Activities to Do. Stories create vivid, lasting images in students' minds. So do hands-on experiments students can perform. Together, these two activities create deep understanding and lasting impressions. The experiments included here require a minimum of equipment and preparation, and can easily be conducted by most primary students.

    Additional Reading. A listing of additional readings on the scientists and the science topics is included to guide further student research. Most of the listed works can be found in the children's library. A few are excellent titles from the adult section. If your library doesn't carry these exact books, I am sure it includes similar ones that will meet the needs of your students.

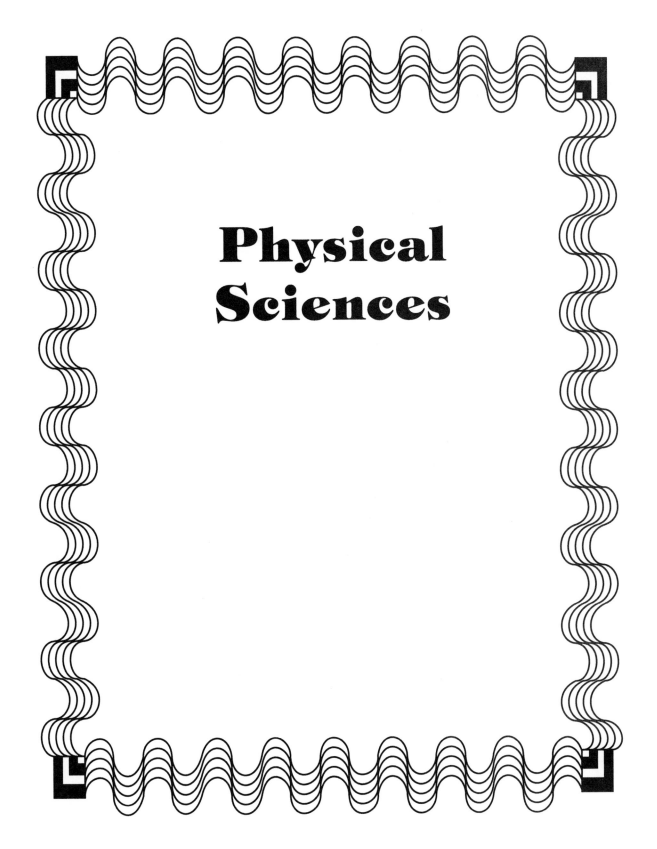

Physical Sciences

Flight

"Launching" a Scientist

A Story of Robert Goddard's First Attempt at Rocketry in 1887

➤ **A Point to Ponder**

A pre-story question to focus student attention and interest on the story's central science theme—What is a force? What force (or push) makes a rocket rise into the air? What forces push on you right now? Is the wind a force? Is sunlight a force? Do your muscles create a force?

➤ **Science Curriculum Links**

This story deals with the physical science concepts of motion and force. What force (or push) makes something go (in this case up)? What force (or pull) holds it down? When something moves vertically, what is the pattern of its motion? Why does it move that way?

Use this story to introduce the study of flight, rockets, or space flight, or as part of a study of motion and the patterns of motion.

➤ **Key Picture-Maker Words**

The following words create mental pictures important to the understanding of this story. However, not all your students may be familiar with each of them. Here are ways to quickly review these words and concepts to ensure that your students get the most out of these moments in science.

1. **Launch:** "To launch" means the same as "to take off" or "to send off," and is normally used with rockets. We say an airplane "takes off," but a rocket is "launched."

   When used to describe what a person does (such as young Bobby Goddard in this story) it means to throw oneself forward, or to spring forward, with great energy and enthusiasm.

   Have you ever "launched" yourself into a project or game? Have you ever launched yourself off a railing, bench, or chair and up into the air?

2. **Force:** A force is strength, energy, or power exerted against an object. Your muscles create force. Electricity creates force. Wind creates force. You apply a force to an object to make it move or to deform it.

    Lay a pencil on a table. One force, gravity, holds it to the table, trying to pull (move) it down to the center of the Earth. How many other forces can you find or create to move this pencil?

    Blow on it. The wind of your breath creates a force that can move the pencil. Push it with your finger, elbow, or nose. In each case your muscles create a force that moves the pencil.

    Burning gasoline in an engine changes chemical force into mechanical force that can move a car and could move the pencil.

    If an iron band were wrapped around the pencil, the magnetic force of a magnet could move it.

    Grab the pencil (or a stick) in both hands and break it. Your muscles exerted a force that deformed the pencil.

    These are all examples of common forces that we create and use every day. See if your students can list other forces that affect their lives.

3. **Static Electricity:** We have all felt static electricity, especially on days with low humidity. Your hair reaches up toward a comb or brush and seems to stand straight up all on its own. The cause? Static electricity that has built up in your body.

    We have all felt a shock or spark jump from a metal doorknob to our hand. This is really static electricity moving from your body to the doorknob and back down into the ground.

    Take clothes out of the dryer at night with the lights off, and you'll see pops and sparks of light as you pull socks and shirts apart. Static electricity built up in the clothes as they tumbled in the dryer.

    Static electricity is any electrical charge that slowly builds up in a single, fixed place, such as your body or your socks in the dryer. Long before humans knew anything about electricity, they knew about and had felt static.

"Launching" a Scientist

Two six-year-old boys played in front of a two-story house in Boston in September 1887. The leaves were just beginning to turn bright yellow and red.

"It won't work," called freckle-faced Percy Long.

"It will too!" insisted his shorter, dark-haired friend.

"You can't fly, Bobby. Only birds fly," yelled Percy.

But Bobby Goddard was not about to back down. "This is called science. You just count once I fly off the porch railing."

"Where are you going?" asked Percy.

"Inside to shuffle. It'll help me fly. You just remember to count!" Bobby opened the front door and ran into the living room. He slid his shoes along the thick wool carpet, shuffling back and forth across the room.

"Hurry up!" called Percy.

"Just a second!" Bobby shuffled two more laps across the living room carpet. "Here I come!" He ran back out the open front door; stepped once on a bench just below the railing; sprang to the railing; and with a mighty leap, launched himself into space. "Count!"

"One . . . two . . ."

THUD! Bobby crashed into the soft dirt of his mother's flower bed below the railing. He crumpled two flower bushes, flattened half a dozen chrysanthemums, and left deep holes where his elbows and knees hit.

Percy laughed so hard he almost fell over. "I told you you couldn't fly."

Bobby sat up and rubbed his sore knee. "Maybe I didn't get enough static electricity." He climbed out of the flowers and back onto the front porch. "I'm going to try it again. This time I'll shuffle more to get more static electricity. So you be ready to count."

Bobby stepped into the house and began to shuffle across the living room carpet again. Back and forth, scraping his shoes across the carpet.

"Here I come!" He raced back onto the front porch. One foot on the bench. One foot on the railing. And into the clear blue sky.

Percy counted. "One . . . two . . . three . . . four . . ."

From *Stepping Stones to Science.* © 1997 Kendall Haven. Teacher Ideas Press. (800) 237-6124.

SMASH! Bobby wiped out two hydrangea bushes as he crashed down and rolled across the grass.

Again Percy laughed. But Bobby jumped to his feet. "Don't laugh. I flew longer that time!"

Percy squeaked to a stop in the middle of a laugh. It was true. Bobby *had* stayed in the air almost twice as long that time.

"Bobby Goddard!" called his mother from the porch. "I've told you a thousand times not to leave the front door open." She looked over the porch railing and gasped, "My land! What have you done to my flowers?"

"He was crashing, Mrs. Goddard," said Percy.

"I was flying, mom," corrected Bobby, glaring at his friend.

"Flying?" exclaimed Mrs. Goddard. "So far you've only managed to fly as far as my flower beds. And right now, young man, you will fix the damage you've done."

Bobby lowered his eyes and softly sighed. "Yes, ma'am."

Bobby's father stepped onto the porch still carrying the daily newspaper. "What's all the commotion out here?" he asked.

"Bobby's been wrecking my flower beds. That's what!" snapped Mrs. Goddard.

"I was flying, dad," insisted Bobby.

"Mostly, he was crashing," said Percy.

Mr. Goddard squatted next to his son. "How were you trying to fly, Bobby?"

"Electricity, dad."

Mr. Goddard nodded. "So that's what all that shuffling across the living room was for. You were building up static electricity. And here I thought you were just wearing out the rug." He thought for a moment. "But why did you think static electricity would help you fly?"

Bobby shrugged. "You told me yesterday that when I shuffle my feet across a rug, electricity *rises* up from the carpet into my feet. You said that's what we call static electricity. So I figured if electricity likes to rise up, if I had some with me when I jumped, maybe it would carry me up with it as it went."

Mr. Goddard clamped both hands over his mouth to cover a laugh.

Bobby looked sad and dejected. "Well, it sort of worked. I flew longer the second time." Then he sighed. "Maybe I just jumped harder."

Mr. Goddard turned to his wife. "Now what do you think of our boy, Fannie? I tell him one thing about electricity and he puts it together with two other ideas and comes up with a science experiment."

Mrs. Goddard shook her head. "What he came up with was destroying my flower bed!"

"What he came up with was mostly crashing," Percy reminded everyone.

Mr. Goddard looked back at his son. "So your experiment was a failure?"

Bobby nodded sadly.

"Good. Failure is how scientists learn," explained his father. "You try something. It flops. That leads you to a better idea. The important thing is to never stop trying. Now before your next try, you might think about what kind of force is strong enough to push something up into the air."

On a cloudy afternoon three days later, Mrs. Goddard climbed the basement stairs with a load of wash and glanced out the kitchen window. She dropped the laundry basket and screamed. Bobby was balanced on top of the high backyard fence. In his hands he held two huge balloons, each much bigger than his head.

"Land sakes! He must be six feet off the ground!" Mrs. Goddard cried. Then she took a great breath and yelled, "Bobby Goddard, you get down from there this instant! . . . But be careful."

She raced out the back door just as Percy Long's countdown reached, "Ready . . . set . . . GO!"

Mrs. Goddard screamed as Bobby jumped high into the air. As he jumped, he loosened his tight grip on the necks of the two fat balloons. Air rushed out the bottom of each balloon with a piercing screech.

Percy counted. "One . . . two . . . three . . . four . . . fi-"

THUD! Bobby crashed to the soft grass.

The whine of his two balloons slowly died away to a faint hiss as the balloons flattened. Bobby sat up and shook his head to stop the world from spinning before his eyes.

His mother rushed over. "What on earth do you think you were doing?" she demanded.

From *Stepping Stones to Science*. © 1997 Kendall Haven. Teacher Ideas Press. (800) 237-6124.

"I was flying, mom," he answered.

"He was crashing again," corrected Percy.

At dinner that night Mr. Goddard asked, "What's this I hear about you trying to fly again?"

"He just about broke his neck, is what he did," said his mother.

"Mostly, he was crashing," said Percy who had stayed for dinner.

"I was using balloons to create force, dad. You taught me that when air rushes out the bottom of a balloon, it pushes the balloon up. I figured they'd take me up with them."

Mr. Goddard smiled. "Did you hear that, Fannie? What do you think of our boy now?"

Softly Bobby asked, "Is this another failure, dad?"

"You just need a bigger force, son. More power. A lot more power. Oh, and maybe it's time to stop sending yourself up with your rockets. Safer for you to watch from the ground. Yup. A few more experiments and a little more power. I think you'll get it."

Forty years later, on March 16, 1926, Robert Goddard launched the world's first liquid-fueled rocket. It rose 50 feet off the ground. By 1937 one of his rockets thundered more than 9,000 feet into the air, and the Space Age began for humankind. In another 25 years rockets regularly roared free of Earth's gravity to place satellites and manned capsules in space. But that's another story.

■　■　■

Follow-Up Activities

Young Robert Goddard struggled to understand a specific kind of motion: lifting something into the air. Through his experiments he searched for a force that would push him up into the air with greater force than the force of gravity that pulled him down. The name for the force that pushes a rocket into the air is "thrust."

Here are some fun, easy, and powerful activities you can do to better understand thrust and gravity (the pushes that make something rise, and the pull that makes it come back down).

Topics to Talk About

1. **Motion**—What is motion? (*Movement resulting from some force acting on an object or body.*) How do you describe motion? (*By measuring the characteristics of the motion: speed, direction, and the change in speed and/or direction over time.*)

2. **Patterns**—How did Bobby move when he jumped from the porch rail or from the fence? (***Up.** He moved up slower and slower and slower. Then he stopped. Then down, faster and faster.* ***Forward.** He always moved forward, but slowed slightly over the time he was in the air.*) Why? What made him move this way? (*Three forces pulled on Bobby's body to make it move this way: gravity, air resistance, and the lift or thrust from his legs.*)

3. **Force**—What forces pushed Bobby up each time? (*Leg muscles on his first jump. Leg muscles and air escaping from two balloons on his second.*) What force pulled him back down? (*Gravity.*) What force slowed his movement through the air? (*Air resistance or drag.*)

Activities to Do

1. Necessary Equipment. Each group of students will need:
   - Several softballs
   - One tape measure per group
   - Copies of "Student Worksheet," page 12

2. Getting off the Ground.

   The force of gravity holds you to the ground. What creates enough thrust to launch you into the air? Many things can create upward power, or thrust. Can *you*? How much thrust do you need in order to lift an object one foot off the floor? Do you need more lift to make that same object rise 100 feet?

From *Stepping Stones to Science.* © 1997 Kendall Haven. Teacher Ideas Press. (800) 237-6124.

Let's try an experiment to see.

- This is an outdoor exercise. All you'll need is one softball per group of students. Start with each softball on the ground in front of the student doing the exercise.

- Reach down and lift the ball chest high. Have you just overpowered gravity? Yes. You applied a greater upward force than gravity exerts downward on the ball. Because the force you applied was greater, the ball rose.

3. Patterns of Motion.

- Throw the ball as close to straight up as you can. Have each group try to describe the ball's pattern of motion. How did it move? How did its direction and speed change? Try several throws. Does the ball follow the same pattern every time? Record your observations for each throw.

- You should have seen that the ball first rises into the sky. As it rises, it slows. Finally it stops. And then it falls again toward Earth, gaining speed as it falls.

- Why? Why didn't it continue to climb? What slowed and then stopped it?

- The answer is, of course, the force of gravity. As soon as you released the ball, there was no longer any force pushing it upwards. However, two forces continued to tug on the ball and slow its upward motion: gravity and air resistance, or drag. As long as the ball is within the gravitational field of the Earth, gravity will continue to pull it down. You can easily overpower the force of gravity. However, the ball will only rise as long as you continue to push the ball upward.

4. Give Yourself a "Lift."

- Can you lift *yourself* with greater force than that with which gravity holds you down? How high can you lift yourself?

Let's do another experiment to see.

- Stand next to a wall on which foot, half-foot, and quarter-foot marks have been drawn, starting from the floor. Jump as high as you can, keeping your legs straight while you are in the air. Have other students watch to see how high your feet rise above the floor. Make three jumps. Record your height for each jump.

- Did each jumping student follow the same pattern of motion that your ball did in step 3 above? Have several students watch as each person jumps to see if everyone's pattern of motion is the same.

- What have you learned? First, that you can overpower gravity. You do it all the time.

- Second, that you only overpower gravity as long as you exert some upward push or thrust. As soon as you let go of a ball, it is no longer being pushed up, and it slows. As soon as your feet leave the floor, your legs are no longer pushing you up, and you slow. However, gravity pulls you down no matter where you are—on the ground or in the air.

- Third, could you overpower gravity enough to lift yourself into space? No, not on a single jump. But you could if you always had something, like a staircase, to push off of. If someone built a staircase fifty miles high, you could climb into space. Of course, it would be hard work to get there; your legs would get tired climbing half a million stairs!

- Let's see how much work you have already performed on your three jumps. Find the average height of your jumps. (Add the height of the three jumps and divide by three.) Multiply this height by your weight. That is a measure of how much work you accomplished. Who in your class performed the most work?

# STUDENT WORKSHEET
for Activities to Do
following a story about **Robert Goddard**

1. Fill in this chart for three throws of a baseball.

Throw #	1	2	3
Time in the Air			
Pattern of Motion			

2. Fill in this chart for your three jumps.

Jump #	1	2	3
Height (inches)			

Average height $\left(\dfrac{\#1 + \#2 + \#3}{3}\right)$ = $\left(\dfrac{ + + }{}\right)$ = _____ inches

Your weight (in lbs) = _____ lbs.

Work = (Average Height X Weight) = (X   ) = _____ inch-lbs

Additional Reading

Good references in the children's library for further reading on rockets and Goddard's experiments include:

Asimov, Isaac. *Rockets, Probes, and Satellites.* Milwaukee, WI: G. Stevens, 1988.

Baird, Ann. *The US Space Camp Book of Rockets.* New York: Morrow Junior Books, 1994.

Coil, Suzanne. *Robert H. Goddard.* New York: Facts on File, 1992.

Cox, Donald. *Rocketry Throughout the Ages.* New York: Winston, 1979.

Daughtery, Charles. *Robert Goddard: Trail Blazer to the Stars.* New York: Macmillan, 1964.

Dewey, Anne. *Robert Goddard, Space Pioneer.* Boston: Little, Brown, 1972.

Farley, Karin. *Robert H. Goddard.* Englewood Cliffs, NJ: Silver Burdett Press, 1991.

Furniss, Tim. *Space Rockets.* Boston: Gloucester Press, 1988.

Hendrickson, Walter. *Who Really Invented the Rocket?* New York: Putnam, 1974.

Lampton, Christopher. *Rocketry: From Goddard to Space Travel.* New York: F. Watts, 1988.

Lehman, Milton. *This High Man: The Life of Robert Goddard.* New York: Farrar, Straus, 1973.

Lomask, Milton. *Robert H. Goddard.* New York: Garrard, 1972.

Maurer, Richard. *Rocket! How a Toy Launched the Space Age.* New York: Crown, 1995.

Quackenbush, Robert. *The Boy Who Dreamed of Rockets.* New York: Parents' Magazine Press, 1978.

Richards, Norman. *Dreamers and Doers.* New York: Morrow Junior Books, 1984.

Verral, Charles. *Robert Goddard: Father of the Space Age.* Englewood Cliffs, NJ: Silver Burdett Press, 1991.

Von Braun, Wernher. *The History of Rockets and Space Travel.* New York: Crowell, 1966.

Consult your librarian for additional titles.

Flight

A "Warped" Idea

A Story of the Wright Brothers' Discovery of Powered Flight in 1903

➤ A Point to Ponder

A pre-story question to focus student attention and interest on the story's central science theme—What force pushes (lifts) an airplane into the air? Why does a plane have to be moving to create lift? Will a balsa wood glider fly higher (get more lift) if you throw it *into* the wind, or *with* the wind?

➤ Science Curriculum Links

This story deals with the physical science themes of motion and lift. How is lift created? How is the motion of flight controlled so that a plane goes where the pilot wants it to? How does airplane flight compare to that of birds?

Use this story to introduce a unit on invention, to introduce the concept of flight, or to illustrate the scientific method of research and development.

➤ Key Picture-Maker Words

The following words create mental pictures important to the understanding of this story. However, not all your students may be familiar with each of them. Here are ways to quickly review these words and concepts to ensure that your students get the most out of these moments in science.

1. **Glider:** A glider is a winged aircraft that has no engine or motor. Gliders are much lighter than powered airplanes and thus are much easier to pull and control, and can take off at much slower speeds.

    The Wright brothers were able to push their gliders into the air simply by having one person hold each wing and jog down the steep slopes of a sand dune into the wind. That slight speed was enough to let the glider and its pilot successfully take off and fly.

2. **Propeller:** Propellers are the large blades mounted in front of old-style airplane engines. They look, spin, and push air in the same way that fan blades do. However, airplane propellers are much bigger, spin much faster, and push air back across a plane's wings with enormous force. Jet airplanes don't have propellers.

3. **Lift:** Lift is the name of the force that makes an airplane rise into the air. The force was named "lift" because it seems to lift an airplane off the ground. Actually, lift is a carefully engineered difference between the air pressure above and below an airplane's wings.

   In the late 1800s scientists discovered that air doesn't push as hard (exert as much pressure) on things around it while it moves faster. The faster the air moves, the less it pushes on the objects around it.

   Scientists figured that if they shaped a wing correctly, they could make the air flowing over its topside move faster than the air flowing along its underside. Air above the wing would push *down* on the wing with a lesser pressure than the air underneath would push *up*. With a greater pressure (or force) pushing up, the wing and plane would be pushed, or lifted, into the air. That is lift, the force that makes all winged aircraft fly.

4. **Sand Dunes:** In some places nature has piled vast stretches of sand. Some of these sand areas are miles wide and many miles long.

   When wind blows across the ocean, it makes waves. A strong wind can build up seemingly endless rows of waves 30, 50, even 100 feet high.

   Wind blowing over sand does the same thing. But these rolling hills of sand don't flatten out when the wind stops, as water in the ocean does. Sand waves remain. When the wind blows again, it blows these sand hills yet higher and steeper, so that most sand areas have become great seas of steeply sloped sand hills, or waves.

   Our name for these rolling seas of sand is "sand dunes." One area of sand dunes is just south of Kitty Hawk, North Carolina. Those are the dunes Orville and Wilbur Wright chose to test their gliders and motorized airplane.

5. **Launch:** "To launch" means the same as to "take off" or "to send off." While the word *launched* is more often used with rockets (we say an airplane "takes off," but a rocket is "launched"), it also is used to mean getting something new to work, to start, or to get under way.

   In this story, the Wright brothers are trying to "launch" their airplane (get it to work and make it fly for the first time) and to "launch" the era of flight for humankind.

6. **Vertical:** Vertical is straight up and down. A ruler held straight up and down is vertical.

   When used to describe motion, "vertical" usually refers to moving straight up. Vertical flight is a difficult and dangerous thing for an airplane to do. The downward pull of gravity slows the plane; its wings stop creating lift force; and the plane becomes unstable and tends to curl into spiraling dives straight back toward Earth.

7. **Stabilize:** Stabilize means to make something steady, or to keep it from moving in a way you don't like. Early manned gliders jumped and bounced all over the sky at the whim of swirling winds. The planes were too unstable to fly. Much of the work that made the Wright brothers successful was their effort to learn how to stabilize an airplane.

   You can easily demonstrate stabilized versus unstabilized flight with your hand. Hold your hand out at shoulder level, fingers extended, palm flat as if the hand were an airplane. Violently shake the hand, pitching it up and down, rocking it side to side, buffeting it about in the sky. This is unstabilized flight. Now steady the hand so that it hovers, motionless in the air. This is stabilized flight.

8. **(Wing) Warp:** Deforming the straight wings of an airplane so that one side curls slightly up and one side curls slightly down is called "wing warp."

   While wing warp is hard to picture in your head, it is easy to demonstrate with a long (18" or more) plastic ruler. Lay an eraser across the middle of the ruler to represent an airplane's body. Hold the ruler with one hand at each end. Rotate your left hand forward and your right hand backward. The eraser airplane remains stationary while both wings warp, one curving up and one curving down. That is what the Wright brothers meant by "wing warp."

9. **Research:** Research is a careful, thoughtful, studious search for fact or truth. Research is what scientists do. Experiments are one way to do research. Research may also be done by reading and comparing various reports and books in the library, or by questioning people with knowledge of a subject.

10. **Discovery:** A discovery is the act of making known something that was not previously known. Isaac Newton discovered gravity, not because he invented or created it, but because he made it known. Columbus discovered the New World. It had always been there, but he made its presence known to Europeans.

    The Wright brothers discovered flight. The necessary techniques had always been there, but they were not known until Orville and Wilbur discovered the secrets of controlled flight.

A "Warped" Idea

William Tate rocked back and forth on the front porch of his general store in the village of Kitty Hawk, North Carolina. It was mid-summer, 1905. His young face, like the wooden buildings around him, seemed worn by the constant salty winds.

Five reporters, one of them from as far away as Washington, D.C., huddled around him. The Wright brothers were up flying again, back in their home town of Dayton, Ohio. Their latest world-record flight covered 25 miles with plenty of turns and loops to show that they and their marvelous aeroplane had conquered the skies. The reporters had come to Kitty Hawk to get the story of how those flying wonders had started.

William leaned forward in his rocker, as if sharing an important secret. "Back in July of 1901, when Wilbur and Orville first showed up, I thought they were crazy. Oh, they were polite and all. But I figured you'd have to be crazy to think man could fly."

One of the reporters asked, "Mr. Tate, show us the sand dunes where it all started."

"Oh, it didn't start *here*," answered William. "The Wright brothers had over two years of research under their belts before they came out here. Ya see, back in the spring of 1899 there were over a dozen others all tryin' to be the first to fly. What put Orville and Wilbur ahead of the rest is the science, the research they did. And *that* started in their bike shop in Dayton. That's where they made the first of their two great discoveries."

* * *

Twenty-six-year-old Wilbur, who was four years older and much taller than Orville, yelled in the back door of their bike shop, "Orville. Come out here. Quick!"

Orville dashed outside to find his brother lying on the small hill rising behind the "Wright Cycling Company," hands tucked behind his head, looking up into the sky. "Wilbur! What are you doing? I got customers in there."

Wilbur pointed up. "Watch these buzzards."

"Are you crazy?"

"Watch what they do with their wings," commanded Wilbur.

Orville shrugged and plopped down into the soft spring grass. Within a minute Orville saw what had captivated Wilbur. "That's amazing! They control their flight just by changing the shape and position of their wings as they glide—not by flapping."

Three things were needed to fly: lift, power, and control. Wing design to create lift was well known. Motors with propellers were readily available for power. But control—making the plane go where you wanted instead of where the wind took it—was a different story. Nobody had figured out how to control an aeroplane once it was in the air.

But Wilbur's buzzards had.

"There. See that?" asked Wilbur. When a left wing tipped up, the right wing tipped down. When one wing curled forward, the other curled back, always moving in opposite directions to each other.

Wilbur jumped up with a wonderful idea. "If we can make an aeroplane's wings warp the same way that bird does, we'll be able to control our flights. Do you still have the long shipping box for the order of inner tubes we received last week?"

Orville ran back into the shop, his customer both gone and forgotten. Rummaging through a dark corner of the store room, he found the square-ended, waist-high cardboard box.

Wilbur took the box from his brother and held it with one hand over each end. "Their wings always move in opposite directions. Watch this." Wilbur turned one hand counterclockwise, and the other clockwise. The box warped into a twist. "See? One wing curls up. One wing curls down. We'll do the same to our aeroplane's wings—warp the wings to give us control of the flight."

* * *

William Tate rocked back in his chair. "That was the beginnin' of the Wright brothers' successful design. But they spent two more years testin' wings before they arrived here with their first full-sized glider. Yup, I said glider. They didn't try a motorized flight until they tested gliders for two more years after that!"

Scribbling notes, one reporter asked, "Why'd they come way out here?"

William gestured at the blowing sand and dust. "Wind. Wind to get the glider up in the air. Yer standin' on one of the windiest spots in America. Well, wind *and* the sand dunes for a soft landing area. I showed 'em down to Kill Devil Hills dunes myself, you know."

The reporters all chuckled. "Why'd they need a soft landing area? They crash a lot?"

"It's not funny," snapped William. "Every crash of that glider meant two, three weeks lost time for repairs, and lost money for replacement parts. The Wright brothers were short on both."

The reporter from the Washington Post thumbed back through his notes. "You said Wilbur and Orville made two great discoveries. Wing warp was the *first*. What was the second?"

William nodded. "Had the second one down at the dunes. I helped. Late September, 1902, it was.

"They set up a tent camp down there. I'd go down in the evenin's. Orville always cooked. Wilbur always washed dishes and kept camp neat. Then Orville'd pull out his harmonica, and Wilbur'd drag out his mandolin and they'd play 'till it got chilly.

"Orville was up flying the glider one day. Wilbur and I launched him. We'd each hold one of the wing tips and run down a steep sand dune until there was enough speed to lift the glider into the air.

"There was a steady wind that afternoon, and Orville shot up like a bird, usin' the wing warp to keep himself nose into the wind, or usin' wing warp to start long, graceful turns. I tell ya, Orville outflew the seagulls that day!

"Then he nosed up too steep and almost stalled. His right wing dipped. He threw the wing warp hard left to level her out. The glider shuddered. Then the tail just kicked around. I stood on the sand watchin'. The glider nosed into a twistin' dive. Orville couldn't pull out. And crash! The glider splintered on the beach.

" 'cept for some bruises, cuts, and some blood on his shirt, Orville was all right. But the glider was wrecked. It was a mighty sad evenin' in camp that night, I tell ya. That is, until Orville sat straight up on his cot, nursing a stiff neck, and called out, 'Wilbur, I know what happened. The tail got lift.'

"And that was their second great discovery. Under some conditions the vertical tail section could act just like a wing and produce lift—only it was lift to the side instead of up and down, ya see. That's what kicked the glider out of control and into a dive.

"All they had to do to fix it was make the tail turn when the glider turned. They hooked the tail to the wing warp controls. When the wing warp eased the glider into a turn, the tail rotated to stabilize and help the turn.

From *Stepping Stones to Science*. © 1997 Kendall Haven. Teacher Ideas Press. (800) 237-6124.

"Those two discoveries gave Orville and Wilbur control of flyin'. And that's why they were the first to fly."

William Tate eased back into his rocker and crossed his arms, with a single, firm nod to announce the end of his story.

"But what of the world's first motorized aeroplane flight, the one on December 17, 1903?" demanded one of the reporters. "That's when history was made."

"Oh, that," sneered Tate. "I s'pose *that's* what'll become famous. Probably even go down in the history books." He shook his head in disgust. "Oh, I mean, it was a pretty thing, and all. Man flying by motor, without relying on the wind. But that was bound to happen 'cause Wilbur and Orville did their homework, their science. The real miracles happened, ya see, in their Ohio bike shop, and in the glider out here on the dunes. Now what *I'm* waitin' for is when flyin' turns practical—ya know, carryin' people and cargo where they need to go. But I s'pose that's another story."

■   ■   ■

Follow-Up Activities

The Wright brothers struggled for years to understand how birds fly and to adapt birdlike principles to their glider and powered airplane designs. Their greatest challenge was control of the plane once it was airborne.

Here are some fun, easy, and powerful activities you can do to better understand the force (lift) that makes a plane fly, and some of the control issues that the Wright brothers had to conquer.

Topics to Talk About

1. **Lift:** What force keeps an airplane in the air? (*A partial vacuum above an airplane's wing caused by having air above the wing travel faster than air just below the wing, which sucks the plane up into the sky.*) How is that force created? (*Speed. The air moving across the wing has to flow at hundreds of miles an hour. That's why airplanes have to race down long runways before they can take off. The pilot is waiting for the plane's engine to create enough speed. Then he can use the plane's wings to lift the plane into the air.*) Is it the same force that pushes a rocket into the sky? (*No. A rocket's engines are similar to a jet airplane's engines. But a jet airplane's engines are small. They can make the plane go forward but aren't powerful enough to drive it up into the air. That's why planes have wings and use the wing's lift to rise into the air. Rockets have no wings to create lift. They must rely on much more powerful rocket engines that are strong enough to drive the rocket into the air and out into space.*)

2. **Control:** How does a plane fly straight? How does it turn? (*Pilots have controls that move small parts of the back side of each wing and that can rotate part of the tail. These control flaps change the shape of each wing and the way that air flows past the wing. This is what lets the pilot control whether the plane flies straight or turns.*) Does a plane control its flight the same way a bird does? (*Not quite. Many of the same ideas found in a bird's wings are used in the design of a plane's wings. But a bird's wings are much more complex and can bend and twist in many more ways than mechanical airplane wings can.*)

Activities to Do

1. Necessary Equipment:
   - One sheet of notebook paper
   - Two thick books of equal size
   - One drinking straw

- One small ball (a golf ball is a good size and weight)

- Scissors, string, and tape

- Copies of "Student Worksheet," page 24

2. Getting a Lift from Air Pressure.

Lift is the name of the force that keeps an airplane in the air. But how is that force created? The Wright Brothers and other early flyers discovered that as air moved faster and faster across a surface (like a wing), it exerted less and less pressure on that surface. If they could make the air flow faster across the top of a wing than across the bottom, there would be less pressure on the top of the wing than on the bottom. Thus, the extra pressure pushing up on the bottom of the wing would make the plane rise.

Sounds goofy, doesn't it? But that's exactly what makes every airplane fly. Let's do two simple experiments to see if you can create that same pressure difference and lift.

- First, lay two equally thick books about four inches apart on a table. Lay a sheet of notebook paper across the space between the books. (See the worksheet illustration to be sure of the setup.) The piece of paper just lays there, right? That's because the force of gravity isn't strong enough to pull the paper down, and air pushes equally hard on both sides.

- Now place the end of a straw just under the front edge of the paper in the middle of the gap between the books and blow through the straw as hard as you can.

- What happened to the paper? It sagged down in the middle, right? Why?

- When you blew, air moved faster across the bottom of the paper than across the top. The faster air moves, the less hard it pushes on objects next to it. That is, the less pressure it exerts. With less air pressure on the bottom than on the top, the paper was pushed down.

- Try placing the end of the straw just above the middle edge of the paper. Now does the paper flutter and seem to rise a little? You have created lift!

3. A Curve Ball Is Really Science.

Have you ever seen a baseball pitcher throw a curve ball? Did you know that air pressure and lift make the ball curve? Let's do an experiment to see if you can create a curve ball.

- Tape the end of a three-foot string to the small ball you collected for this experiment. Tape the string's other end to the top edge of a table. The ball must not touch the floor, but the lower it hangs from the table the better.

- Pull the ball back away from the table and let it go. It swings back and forth in a straight line, right? Air pressure on both sides of the ball is the same.

- Before you pull the ball back and release it again, twist the string 75 to 100 times in a counterclockwise direction. Now pull the ball and twisted string back and release it.

- Did it swing back and forth in a straight line this time? No. Why not?

- Your ball is now moving in two ways. It is swinging forward as it did before, and it is spinning on its axis. As the ball spins, it drags a thin layer of air around with it, spinning around and around in a circle with the ball. Picture this air flowing around the ball just like a satellite spins around the Earth. As this air flows around the ball, on one side it flows forward (from back to front), while it flows backward (from front to back) on the other side.

- As the ball swings forward, air rushes past on both sides. On both sides, air flows past the ball from front to back (backward). See the worksheet illustration of this air movement.

- Now think of what happens when these two motions happen at the same time. On one side the air motion from the spinning and **the motion** from the ball's swing move in the same direction (backward). The air moves faster on this side and air pressure is lower.

- On the other side, air motion from the ball's **spin** flows in the opposite direction from air motion caused by the ball's **swing**. On this side air piles up, and its motion is slowed. As the air motion slows on this side, air pressure builds higher.

- With higher air pressure on one side and lower pressure on the other, the ball is pushed to one side. We say that it "curves." It is **really** just lift that pushes the ball to one side in the same way lift pushes the wings of an airplane into the sky.

# STUDENT WORKSHEET
for Activities to Do
following a story about **The Wright Brothers**

---

1. Getting A "Lift."

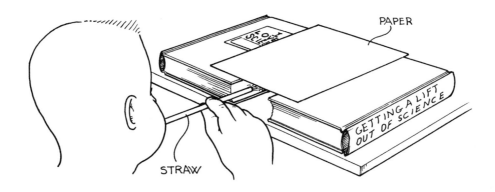

2. A Curve Ball Is Really Science.

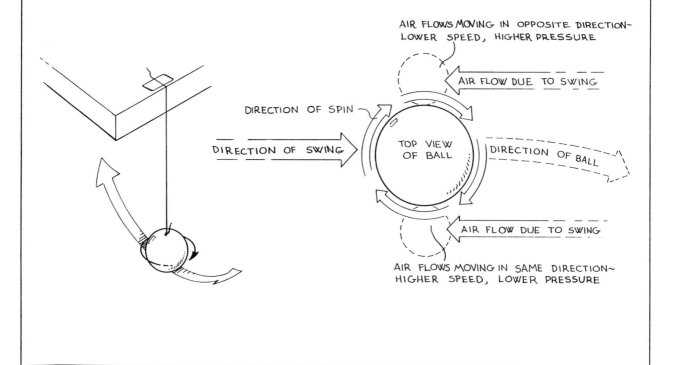

Additional Reading

Good references in the children's library for further reading on flight, on airplanes, and on the Wright brothers' experiments include:

Ash, Russell. *The Wright Brothers*. London: Wayland Press, 1974.

Combs, Harry. *Kill Devil Hill: Discovering the Secrets of the Wright Brothers*. Boston: Houghton Mifflin, 1979.

Crouch, Tom. *The Bishop's Boys: A Life of Wilbur and Orville Wright*. New York: W. W. Norton, 1989.

Freedman, Russell. *The Wright Brothers: How They Invented the Airplane*. New York: Holiday House, 1991.

Geibert, Ron. *Kitty Hawk and Beyond*. Dayton, OH: Wright State University Press, 1989.

Glimes, Carroll. *The Wright Brothers: Pioneers of Flight*. New York: F. Watts, 1978.

Graves, Charles. *The Wright Brothers*. New York: Putnam, 1973.

Hallion, Richard. *The Wright Brothers: Heirs of Prometheus*. Washington, DC: Smithsonian Institution Press, 1978.

Hook, Jason. *The Wright Brothers*. New York: Bookwright Press, 1989.

Howard, Fred. *Wilbur and Orville: A Biography of the Wright Brothers*. New York: Knopf, 1987.

Schulz, Walter. *Will and Orv*. Minneapolis, MN: Carolrhoda Books, 1991.

Sproule, Anna. *Los Hermanos Wright*. Madrid: Ediciones SM, 1990.

Walsh, John. *One Day at Kitty Hawk: The Untold Story of the Wright Brothers and the Airplane*. New York: Crowell, 1975.

Westcott, Lynanne. *Wind and Sand: The Story of the Wright Brothers at Kitty Hawk*. New York: H. N. Abrams, 1983.

Consult your librarian for additional titles.

Physics

The "Fall" of Galileo

A Story of Galileo's Discovery in 1598 of How Objects Fall

➤ **A Point to Ponder**

A pre-story question to focus student attention and interest on the story's central science theme—If you drop a bowling ball and a marble side by side, which would fall faster? What if you dropped a bowling ball and a feather? What about dropping a feather and a piece of paper? Why do you think the results would be different?

➤ **Science Curriculum Links**

This story deals with the physical science principles of motion and gravity. When something falls, what is the pattern of its motion? Do all objects fall the same? What forces control the way something falls?

Use this story as part of a study of gravity, of motion, of patterns of motion, or of famous scientists.

➤ **Key Picture-Maker Words**

The following words create mental pictures important to the understanding of this story. However, not all your students may be familiar with each of them. Here are ways to quickly review these words and concepts to ensure that your students get the most out of these moments in science.

1. **Pendulum:** A pendulum is more easily shown than described. A tetherball on a rope can act as a pendulum. Any disk or spherical weight suspended on a rope, chain, or rod can also be a pendulum.

   Bring a pendulum to class and *gently* swing it back and forth for your students. To act as a true pendulum, the weight should not swing more than about 15° off vertical. Pendulums are useful because the period of each swing (the time it takes to travel from the top of its arc on one side to the other) remains constant. Each swing takes exactly as long as every other swing. Pendulums are thus a reliable and accurate way to record the passage of time.

2. **Experiment:** An experiment is a test, trial, or procedure carried out under controlled conditions in order to discover some unknown value, effect, concept, or law.

   We all regularly conduct informal experiments, or tests. When your students were still babies they experimented with how to stand and walk. Their first attempts, or experiments, on how to control and direct their leg and body muscles and mimic the walking motion of their parents always failed. They collapsed back to the floor. From each failed experiment they learned more about what would and wouldn't work, until one experimental try finally succeeded.

   An experiment is *any* planned test carried out while trying to discover something. Have your students think of other experiments they have conducted, other trial-and-error learning they have undertaken, even though at the time they didn't know they were conducting experiments. (Writing, reading, and riding a bicycle are all examples of what could be experiments.)

3. **Cannonball:** Modern cannonballs are shaped like bullets, long cylinders pointed at the front and filled with chemicals that explode on impact. That was not always the case. Cannonballs originally were solid metal spheres ranging in size from small ones (slightly bigger than your fist) to big brutes more than twice the size of a bowling ball. It was this type of cannonball that Galileo dropped in his famous experiment. Bring in a bowling ball (or even a basketball, volleyball, or tetherball) to fix the look and size of a cannonball in your students' minds.

4. **Leaning Tower of Pisa:** When this tower was built for a prince in Pisa, Italy, it was an ordinary, vertical, round tower. Over time, the ground under one side of the tower settled, tilting the tower's foundation. The tower leaned farther and farther out with each passing decade. It has become famous because it never collapsed even though it stands at a sharp angle and because, like one angled tree trunk in a forest of vertical pines, it sticks out like a sore thumb.

   Galileo used this tower for his experiment because he could drop his cannonballs from the top and not have to worry about them brushing against the tower's side as they fell.

   Here's a simple way to make the look of this tower vivid for your students. Stand four pencils vertically in a row on a table. Have two students help you by holding these pencils. You hold a fifth pencil in this row but slant your pencil at about a 15° angle (roughly one-sixth of a 90°, or right, angle). Your pencil represents the Leaning Tower of Pisa.

5. **Bricks:** Many of your students will be familiar with common red bricks. Some may not. Bring one in and let them see, touch, and hold it before you tell this story. They must know what a brick looks and feels like to successfully visualize Galileo's experiment.

The "Fall" of Galileo

Twenty-five-year-old mathematics professor Galileo Galilee stood before his class at the University of Pisa, Italy, one cloudy afternoon in the spring of 1598. He held out two bricks for them to see—one in each hand, as if he were weighing and comparing them. "Students, I have been watching pendulums swing back and forth. I have watched them very carefully. . . ."

"What's a pendulum?" whispered Ferdinand Bastillo, a 15-year-old student from Spain.

Enricco Buscanti, a 16-year-old from Rome, whispered back, "A pendulum is a ball at the end of a chain or metal rod that swings back and forth."

Ferdinand nodded. "Oh, you mean like in the town square clock. Tick, tock. Tick, tock."

Galileo glared at his students and "hurrumphed!" for silence. "The motion of those pendulums has shown me something about how all objects fall."

Ferdinand asked. "But Professor Galileo, pendulums don't fall. They just swing back and forth."

"You haven't watched pendulums closely enough," scolded Galileo. "They fall. Each time they reach the top of one swing, they *fall* back down to start the next swing."

"Pendulums fall?" repeated Enricco, not sure he had heard correctly.

"Silence!" snapped Galileo. "Pendulums *fall*. After watching their fall very carefully, I have decided that every scientist in the world is wrong."

The class gasped, "All of them? Wrong?!" They looked as frightened as if he had said the world was ending.

Galileo smiled. He knew his class would react this way. He enjoyed surprising them. "Students, I can prove what I say. Watch."

Galileo smugly climbed up onto his desk. "Think, class. What did Aristotle say about falling objects?"

They all knew each of Aristotle's teachings. Aristotle said that heavier objects fall faster because they weigh more. More weight meant a greater pull to the Earth. Ever since, every scientist had agreed with Aristotle.

Galileo held out his hands to stop them. "But Aristotle is wrong. All objects, heavy or light, fall at the same speed. *Really* watch this time. Watch this fall very carefully."

From *Stepping Stones to Science*. © 1997 Kendall Haven. Teacher Ideas Press. (800) 237-6124.

In one hand Galileo picked up one of the bricks he held before. With his other hand he picked up *two* bricks that he had cemented together. This new double-brick was thus more than twice as heavy as the single brick.

Galileo asked, "If Aristotle is right, will the heavier brick fall faster?"

Every student nodded. Of course it would. Heavier objects fell faster. Every scientist said so.

"Watch closely!" bellowed Galileo.

The ring of students actually held their breath as Galileo held out the single brick and the double brick, both at eye level. The room was graveyard quiet.

Galileo released the bricks. Smash! The blows to the floor echoed around the room.

Galileo looked down at his students. "Did the heavier brick fall faster and land first?"

Still wide-eyed, the students nodded. Then Ferdinand scratched his head and shrugged. "Well, it *might* have fallen faster. It all happened so fast. . . . Wasn't it supposed to fall faster?"

Galileo stomped his foot. "NO! Think, students. What did your eyes see?"

Barely above a whisper, Enricco said, "Uhhh . . . that when you drop bricks they dent the floor?"

Exasperated, Galileo demanded the bricks be handed back up to him. "Everyone get down on your hands and knees and look, really look this time! Believe only what your eyes show you."

Galileo held out a single brick in one hand and the double brick in his other. He let them fall. Smash! The bricks dented the old wooden floor. "Did the heavy brick fall faster?" he demanded.

The class shook their heads. No, it had not. They landed together.

"Again!" cried Galileo. His students stared as Galileo again dropped the bricks. Crash!

"Did the heavy brick fall faster?" No. Again the bricks landed together.

Galileo smiled. "I told you everyone was wrong. I noticed that large and small pendulums all fall, or swing, at the same rate. That means that all objects must fall at the same rate, no matter how much they weigh."

"Wow," whispered Ferdinand.

From *Stepping Stones to Science.* © 1997 Kendall Haven. Teacher Ideas Press. (800) 237-6124.

That evening a friend and fellow teacher, Ostilio Ricci, found Galileo still testing, comparing the fall of his bricks from different heights. As Galileo described his experiments, Ostilio gasped, "Every scientist? Wrong?!"

Galileo sighed. "Not you too. Watch. The truth will speak for itself. If I show you the experiment, you will have to believe."

Galileo leapt onto his desk and held out a single brick in one hand, the double brick in the other. "Watch their fall carefully," he instructed, and released the bricks. Crash! "Now, Ostilio, did the heavier brick fall faster as Aristotle said it would? Yes, or no?" It sounded more like a demand than a simple question.

Sheepishly Ostilio looked down at the floor. "Well . . . maybe. It *might* have."

Galileo pounded his fist on his desk in frustration. "Use your eyes, man! Believe only what you can see." Again Galileo dropped the bricks. And again, and again, until the floor around his desk was ringed with gouges and dents.

"Enough!" cried Ostilio. But Ostilio was a cautious scientist. He still had doubts. He would need more than one experiment with a couple of bricks before he would dare to question the teachings of Aristotle. "I admit you are right. *This* double brick falls at the same rate as *this* single brick. Still, I can not so easily believe every other scientist in the world is completely wrong. Search for another explanation, my friend."

Galileo realized that dropping two bricks from his desk wasn't dramatic enough to make the world believe. He needed a bigger, more exciting experiment. But what?

His search led him to the top of the famed Leaning Tower of Pisa with two cannonballs, one roughly ten pounds, the other about one pound. An eager crowd of students, onlookers, and skeptical professors and priests formed a thick circle 200 feet below.

Galileo held the balls over the edge of the tower. In a loud voice he called down to the crowd. "This experiment will be the final test of whether Aristotle's or my 'Theory of Falling Objects' is correct. From such a great height there can be no mistake, no doubt."

Would the heavy cannonball fall faster, as Aristotle claimed, or would both balls fall at the same speed, as Galileo claimed?

From *Stepping Stones to Science.* © 1997 Kendall Haven. Teacher Ideas Press. (800) 237-6124.

Galileo dropped the balls. The crowd stood hushed and stared as they fell. Down, down they whistled and thud—thud! The two balls smashed to the ground 191 feet below at almost the same instant. Galileo was right. The cannonballs had spoken. The evidence was clear.

But the world in 1598 was neither ready nor willing to hear the truth that Galileo's cannonballs spoke as they dropped from the Leaning Tower of Pisa. Some claimed he used magic. Some said it was a trick. Some said he cheated.

No one believed him.

Still, Galileo's work on falling objects became the foundation from which another well-known scientist, Sir Isaac Newton, was able to build upon to make his own famous discovery. But that's another story.

■   ■   ■

Follow-Up Activities

Professor Galileo Galilee struggled to understand how objects really fall. Does the greater weight of a heavy object create a greater force that pulls it toward the Earth faster? Or is an object's weight meaningless, so that all objects fall at the same rate?

Galileo's study was made more difficult because he had no more accurate way to measure time than his own pulse rate. How could he accurately measure the fall of any object if his own heartbeat was his only marker of time?

Here are some fun, easy, and powerful activities you can do to better understand the concepts controlling *how* an object falls, the forces *making* it fall, and the forces *fighting against* that fall, or pushing up on a falling object.

Topics to Talk About

1. **Pendulums**: What is a pendulum? (*A swinging weight suspended by a rod, wire, chain, rope, or string.*) What makes pendulums swing back and forth? (*Gravity. To start a pendulum, you lift the pendulum weight along a circular arc while keeping its chain or rod straight and taught, and let the pendulum weight fall.*) Have you ever seen a pendulum? Where and how do we use pendulums today? (*Grandfather clocks and museum displays on the rotation of the Earth are two common places. See how many you can find.*)

2. **Gravity**: What force makes you fall when you trip? (*Gravity*) What makes rain fall? A rock? An apple? (*All gravity*) Does the same force make everything fall? (*Yes*) What is that force? (*Gravity*) What is gravity? (*A universal attractive force between any two objects. The strength of this force is related to the mass [weight] of the two objects, and inversely related to the distance between them. The bigger two objects are, the stronger the gravitational pull between them. The farther apart they are, the weaker the gravitational force.*) Where would you have to be for that force not to affect you? (*Space. The reason you are weightless in space is because you are too far from the Earth for its gravity to pull you down.*)

Activities to Do

1. Necessary Equipment. Each group of students will need:
   - One rubber eraser or chalkboard eraser
   - One piece of cardboard (8½" by 11" is best)
   - One sheet of facial tissue
   - One wooden pencil
   - Copies of "Student Worksheet," page 35

2. Patterns of Falling.

Can you describe *how* things fall? That is, can you describe the pattern of a falling object's motion? Do all falling objects following the same pattern?

Let's try an experiment and see.

- Have one student drop an eraser from one hand and a piece of cardboard from the other while carefully standing on a desk with the help of a teacher or other adult. The "dropper" must not toss, throw, or flip either eraser or cardboard, but simply hold them out and let them fall. One student should watch the dropper to make sure both objects are dropped at the same instant.

- The other students should carefully watch as both objects fall. Can you describe how each object moved as it fell? Did they fall at the same speed? With the same pattern of motion?

- Have the dropper drop both objects again. Did they follow the same pattern of motion each time? Can you describe those patterns? Write down your conclusions on the worksheet.

- Here are some questions that might help you. Did the eraser travel at the same speed all the time it was in the air, or did it speed up (or slow down) as it fell toward the floor? Did it fall in a straight line, or did it curve? Did it always follow the same pattern? When was the eraser moving the slowest? When did it move the fastest?

- Did your group find that the eraser moved the slowest just as it was released from the dropper's hand, that it traveled the fastest just before it hit the floor, and that it continuously sped up as it fell along a straight line from the dropper's hand to the floor?

- What pattern did the cardboard follow? Why was it different from the pattern of the eraser?

3. Do All Objects Really Fall the Same?

Gravity, of course, is the force that pulls all objects toward Earth when they fall. If gravity were the *only* force pulling on a falling object, all objects would fall in exactly the same way. But *do* all objects fall with the same pattern of motion?

Let's continue our experiment to see.

- This time have your group's dropper release a pencil and a sheet of facial tissue. Which falls faster? Why? Do you think the pencil fell following the same pattern of motion as did the eraser? Why did the facial tissue fall more slowly?

- What's going on? Why don't all objects fall at the same speed and in the same way as Galileo said they would? Was Galileo wrong? Does some force besides gravity push on falling objects and affect the way they fall?

From *Stepping Stones to Science*. © 1997 Kendall Haven. Teacher Ideas Press. (800) 237-6124.

- The answer is air, or air resistance. Galileo wasn't wrong. It's just that the objects he dropped were so heavy and dense that air resistance was too small a force to affect their fall, and too small for him to measure. But the air through which every object falls pushes up on that object, just as gravity pulls it down.

- What is air resistance? Wave your hand quickly through the air. Feel the air rush past your fingers? You had to push that air aside so that your hand could pass through. The force required to push air aside is a measure of the air's resistance. Air resistance increases both when the size of an object increases (the size of a piece of cardboard is big compared to the size of a pencil) and as the speed of the object increases. (Airplanes traveling at 500 miles an hour have a big problem with air resistance. You do not when walking at two or three miles an hour.)

- Your weight is a measure of how hard gravity pulls you down toward the Earth. The same is true for any other object. When the force of gravity is small (as with a featherlight facial tissue) and the object's size is large (as with the facial tissue or a piece of cardboard), the upward push of air resistance is large enough to slow the object's fall.

- That's why your cardboard and facial tissue fell more slowly. It wasn't that gravity pulled on them differently. It was that air resistance was larger for these two objects and so had a greater effect on their fall.

4. Timing Galileo's Way.

If you had to time some event (like how long it took a squirrel to run up a tree), what would you use? A digital wristwatch? A wall clock? Would you call "time" on the telephone? What if none of these things were available? (When Galileo was conducting his experiments, they weren't.) How could you still measure time?

You could measure large amounts of time (an hour or more) by watching a sundial, the movement of stars, or the creep of shadows. But what about small amounts of time? How would you measure 15 seconds without any timepiece at all? How would you compare two events that each took about 15 seconds to see which was faster?

You could count. (One thousand and one, one thousand and two. . .) But you'd never be sure that your counting remained even and accurate. Can you think of another way to time that's always available and more reliable and consistent?

What about your pulse (heartbeat)? Early researchers all used their own pulse beat to compare the time for different events.

- Try timing several events with your own pulse. Have one student walk briskly around the classroom. Everyone else should time this lap using their own pulse beat. Now have a second and then a third student walk around the room while everyone times their laps. Which student walked fastest? Does everyone agree? What makes timing this way difficult? Aren't you glad we have more convenient and accurate ways to measure the passage of time?

# STUDENT WORKSHEET
for Activities to Do
following a story about **Galileo Galilee**

1. The Pattern of a Fall.

	SPEED (Fast, Med., or Slow)	PATTERN OF MOTION As It Fell	AIR RESISTANCE (High, Med., or Low)
Eraser			
Cardboard			
Pencil			
Feather			

2. Timing Galileo's Way.

	Student	# of heartbeats to walk around the room
1.		
2.		
3.		

Additional Reading

Good references in the children's library for further reading on pendulums, on how objects fall, and on Galileo's experiments include:

Barley, George. *Galileo's Children.* New York: Arcade, 1990.

Bernkoph, Michael. *The Sciences of Galileo.* New York: Regents, 1983.

Bixby, M. *The Universe of Galileo and Newton.* New York: American Heritage Books, 1964.

Branley, Franklin. *Gravity Is a Mystery.* New York: Crowell, 1986.

Cavelin, Maurice. *The Natural Philosophy of Galileo.* Cambridge, MA: MIT Press, 1974.

Drake, Stillman. *Galileo.* New York: Hill and Wang, 1980.

———. *Galileo at Work.* Chicago: University of Chicago Press, 1978.

Fermi, Lauri. *Galileo and the Scientific Revolution.* New York: Basic Books, 1981.

Finocchiaro, Maurice. *Galileo and the Art of Reason.* Boston: D. Reidel Publishing, 1980.

Fisher, Leonard. *Galileo.* New York: Macmillan, 1992.

Haines, Gail. *Which Way Is Up?* New York: Atheneum, 1987.

Hitzeroth, Deborah. *Galileo Galilee.* San Diego, CA: Lucent Books, 1992.

Hummel, Charles. *The Galileo Connection.* Downers Grove, IL: InterVarsity Press, 1986.

Marcus, Rebecca. *Galileo and Experimental Science.* New York: F. Watts, 1961.

McTavish, Douglas. *Galileo.* New York: Bookwright Press, 1991.

Parker, Steve. *Galileo and the Universe.* New York: HarperCollins, 1992.

Reston, James. *Galileo: A Life.* New York: HarperCollins, 1994.

Ronan, Colin. *Galileo.* New York: Putnam, 1974.

Suggett, Martin. *Galileo and the Birth of Modern Science.* Hove, England: Wayland, 1981.

Consult your librarian for additional titles.

Physics

A "Bee Line" to Physics

A Story of Shirley Jackson's Early Attempts to Study
Matter, Energy, and Motion in 1955

➤ A Point to Ponder

A pre-story question to focus student attention and interest to the story's central science theme—What is physics? Do you have to be in a special place to study physics? Have you ever studied physics while you thought you were doing something else?

➤ Science Curriculum Links

This story deals with the physical science themes of matter and motion. How do we describe matter? How do we describe motion and the pattern of motion that a particle of matter follows?

Use this story to introduce the study of physics (the study of matter and energy), of female scientists, or of experimental science.

➤ Key Picture-Maker Words

The following words create mental pictures important to the understanding of this story. However, not all your students may be familiar with each of them. Here are ways to quickly review these words and concepts to ensure that your students get the most out of these moments in science.

1. **Mason Jar:** A mason jar is more easily shown than described. Bring one in, if you can, and let it stand in plain sight while you tell the story.

    A mason jar is a wide-mouth glass jar used especially for home canning. They normally have a two-part metal lid—a thin metal plate that lies across the jar's open top, and a metal ring that screws down to hold the plate in place.

    In this story, Shirley Jackson unscrews the rings of two mason jars and then places the jars mouth-to-mouth before sliding out the metal plate lids.

2. **Laboratory:** A laboratory is any place equipped for, or providing opportunity for, scientific study and testing.

   Can a classroom be a laboratory? Can a bedroom be a laboratory? Can a sand box or playground be a lab? Can *any* place become a laboratory?

   The answer is "yes" to each of these questions. What makes a place a laboratory is planning to use it for scientific study and then equipping the place with what you need for that study.

3. **Hovered:** Hummingbirds hover in front of a flower. Helicopters hover over the ground when they sit, motionless, in the air.

   To hover means to flutter, suspended in air, in one place. What else can hover? What have you seen hovering?

   As used in this story "hover" also means to hang in a state of uncertainty, to be unsure of what to do.

   Early in this story, bees "hover" in the middle of a jar. See if both meanings for hover fit with what you think is happening to these bees.

4. **Physics:** Physics is the science that studies matter and energy and the interaction of the two. Does that mean that you could look at anything and still study physics?

   Yes. If you look at how a bird *behaves*, you're studying biology. But if you study how a bird's wings convert energy into motion, you're actually studying physics.

   If you study how to design a building, it's architecture. If you study what basic materials make up a building and the properties of those materials, it's physics.

   Everything in the world (including the world itself) is made up of matter. Everything uses energy. If what you study is matter and energy themselves, you are studying physics.

   In this story young Shirley Jackson studies bees. But because she's trying to understand the basic building blocks of the matter that makes up a bee, and how a bee converts matter (food) into energy (motion), not bee behavior or the life cycle of a bee, she's studying physics.

5. **Matter:** The next question is, "What is matter?" Matter is the stuff, the substance, that makes up every physical object. Your body is made up of matter. So is your chair and the floor underneath you. So are the trees, birds, and sky outside the window.

    When physicists study matter, they try to break it down to its tiniest pieces and examine the patterns of how those pieces stick together to make the whole.

    A brick wall is a good example. From a distance you could say, "It's just a wall." But if you look closer, you see that the wall is made up of lots of individual bricks. Now you can say, "It's really a bunch of bricks put together in a pattern that shapes them into a wall," and study the pattern of how individual bricks fit together to make a brick wall.

    But if you look still closer, you see that the wall is made up of bricks with mortar all around them to hold the bricks together. If you look even closer you find that mortar is really a mixture of grains of cement, sand, and water that seem to glue themselves together. You also find that each brick is really made up of countless tiny grains of clay that have been pressed together to form a solid brick.

    If you had a powerful microscope, you could finally look inside each grain of clay, sand, and cement to find that they are each made up of countless smaller particles of matter, all locked together in a particular pattern that is unique to sand, clay, or cement.

    You could do the same thing with the wooden seat of your chair. At first glance it looks like just a piece of wood. But what makes up a piece of wood? Look close and you'll see grain patterns in the wood and find individual fibers of wood, all locked together to make the wood hard and strong.

    But what makes up an individual fiber of wood? With a microscope you find that a long wood fiber is made up of elongated individual cells. And what is each cell made of? And so on and so on, until you have broken a wooden chair seat down to the most basic elements of matter that make it up. That is physics.

6. **Molecule and Atom:** Grains, flecks, drops, specks, and dabs are the smallest particles of matter we can see with our eyes. But there are smaller building blocks to all matter: molecules and atoms.

    The smallest particle of any substance (wood, sand, water, potato, or hair) that still retains the properties of that substance is a molecule. Every molecule of cotton acts like cotton. Every molecule of water acts like water.

In turn, molecules are made up of atoms. An atom is the smallest particle of one of the basic 100-plus chemical elements that make up the world. Every atom of oxygen is identical to every other oxygen atom. Every atom of hydrogen matches every other hydrogen atom. This is also true for every atom of gold, silver, carbon, etc.

When atoms are combined, they make a molecule that no longer acts like the individual elements, but rather like the new substance that the molecule has become.

For example, every molecule of water has one hydrogen atom and two oxygen atoms. Each molecule acts like water, a liquid. If you tore it apart into individual atoms, they would act like hydrogen and oxygen (both gases), and not act like water at all. Oxygen is the gas you have to breathe to stay alive.

Here is an image that may help your students understand the relationship between molecules and atoms. One person is a baseball player. You can't cut a person up into parts and still expect that person to play baseball. Nine players combine to make up a new thing called a "baseball team." An individual player is like an atom. Nine players linked together as a "team" is like a molecule.

A "Bee Line" to Physics

Ten-year-old Shirley Jackson squatted in the crawl space under the back porch of her family's small house in Washington, D.C. The deep shadows and cool dirt held off the worst of the heat in this August of 1955. Outside, a fierce summer sun beat down on the city. Heat waves shimmered up from the blacktop on Georgia Street where the Jacksons lived. Kids laughed and squealed down at the corner, where someone had opened a fire hydrant, blasting jets of cool water out across the intersection.

But Shirley noticed neither the heat nor the noise outside. She hunched over two glass mason jars she called her "laboratories." A dozen honeybees buzzed back and forth inside one jar. Some darted across the jar to crash into the clear glass sides and lid; several hovered in the safe middle of the jar. Three walked across the jar's bottom, groping for a way out.

Eight yellow jackets did the same in the other jar.

These were not the first jars of bees that pigtailed Shirley had collected at the neighborhood park. She loved to listen to the ferocious buzzing of bee wings and the occasional bonk of a startled bee smashing headlong into the sides of the glass jar. She loved to watch the patterns and buzzing motion of these small yellow and black bundles.

"Whatcha doin' under there, Shirley?" It was Shirley's father coming back from hauling a load of trash to the dumpster. His T-shirt was soaked with sweat.

"I'm doing a physics experiment," answered Shirley.

Mr. Jackson chuckled. "*Physics!* Pretty fancy word for a young girl."

"I'm almost a *fifth* grader!" she answered without looking up. Then added, "Physics is what our teacher said scientists study."

Mr. Jackson wiped the sweat out of his eyes and leaned over his daughter's shoulder. "What kind of experiment you doin' with your mama's mason jars?"

Shirley began to carefully unscrew one of the jar lids. "I want to see what happens when I mix honeybees and yellow jackets."

Mr. Jackson peered closer. "I thought yellow jackets *were* bees."

"No, Daddy. Yellow jackets are wasps. I read that at the library."

Mr. Jackson scrunched up his face. "Now you be careful, Shirley, or some of your experiment's liable to buzz out and sting you."

From *Stepping Stones to Science.* © 1997 Kendall Haven. Teacher Ideas Press. (800) 237-6124.

With the first lid unscrewed but still sitting loose on top of its jar, Shirley began to unscrew the second lid. "I want to see if they act different once they're mixed together. Our teacher said that's what scientists do."

"Study *bees*?" asked her father.

"NO. They study matter and energy and motion."

Shirley paused and looked around at her father. "Daddy, is it okay for me to be a scientist?"

He smiled and placed his hand on her shoulder. "Why wouldn't it be all right for my little brainchild to be anything she wants?"

She whispered, " 'Cause I'm a girl . . . and I'm black. Our teacher said she didn't think there were any black women scientists."

Mr. Jackson squirmed in next to his daughter. "When I got my job at the post office there weren't many blacks there, either. Now we got lots. If there aren't any black women scientists *now*, it just means you get to be the first. Don't ever let anyone say you can't."

Shirley smiled and nodded. "Then I *am* going to be a scientist. You just watch!" She turned the yellow jacket jar upside down and set it on top of the jar with bees.

Mr. Jackson scrambled back from his daughter. "Shirley, you be careful! Those are ornery cusses you got there."

Slowly Shirley slid out both lids. Wasps and bees met at the border of the two mason jars. Instantly the buzzing increased to a frantic pitch. Wasps dove for honeybees. Bees fled, crashing into the glass. Several bees grouped together and drove at one of the wasps, stingers bared. Stung and beaten warriors from both sides dropped to the glass bottom of the jar.

"Ooooowweee!" Mr. Jackson whistled. "You got a regular war in there, Shirley!"

Shirley watched, fascinated, unable to pull her eyes away from the wild, buzzing motion.

"What'd you say you were studyin'?" asked her father.

"Physics," answered Shirley, still staring at her experiment.

"Don't you mean biology, or war? Something like that?"

"No, Daddy. Physics. That's the study of what makes up the world. It's where you study matter and motion and energy. My teacher taught me that. Those bees are made of the same molecules and atoms that we are. Scientists call it *matter*. The matter is just put together in a different pattern to make a bee. And look at how much energy and motion they get with just their little bits of matter!"

"Well you just watch out that some of that 'matter and motion' don't sneak out and sting you."

Inside her jars only two yellow jackets and one honeybee still wearily buzzed back and forth, desperately searching for an escape. All the rest lay dead or dying on the bottom.

"That was something to watch," said her father, slowly shaking his head and thinking of the wonder of nature and the miracle of life.

"It sure was," whispered Shirley, thinking of atoms and molecules and how they made up everything in the whole world.

Three days later Mrs. Jackson stepped through the back gate struggling with two heavy bags of groceries. There sat Shirley on the bottom step, studying a row of jars before her.

"Shirley Ann! What are you doing with all my mason jars?"

"Not *all*, Mom. I'm only using five. It's another physics experiment."

Mrs. Jackson peered through her glasses, past her scrunched-up nose, and around her grocery bags. "Are those bees? You get those bees right on out of here, young lady! I don't want bees nesting around my house."

With one of the long, disgusted sighs children save for the times parents don't show the intelligence God gave a grasshopper, Shirley said, "Mommmmm. They can't get out. They're trapped in these jars. And it's an experiment."

Five bees flitted back and forth in each jar. But on the floor of each jar lay a different pile of food—flecks of deep orange clover pollen in one, a mound of sugar in a second, a thin layer of honey in a third, grass in a forth, and a tall pyramid of salt in the last. "I'm studying how the bees act with different foods."

Her mother glared angrily at her. "Why don't you make it part of your experiment to see what happens when you move every last one of those bees on out of here?"

From *Stepping Stones to Science*. © 1997 Kendall Haven. Teacher Ideas Press. (800) 237-6124.

Shirley pulled her bright, black eyes away from her jars. "It's just physics, Mom. Matter turns into energy; energy turns into matter. But the atoms stay the same all the time no matter what you do. I read that in a library book. I want to see how bees use these different kinds of food, or matter, to make energy, and also to make more bee matter."

Mrs. Jackson wagged a thick finger at her daughter. "Shirley Ann Jackson. I'll tell you what 'matters.' I want those bees out of here *now*!"

Eighteen years later Shirley Jackson became the first African American awarded a doctoral degree from the famed Massachusetts Institute of Technology (MIT). Since then she has become a renowned physicist working for the Bell Laboratories in New Jersey, where she develops computerized mathematical models of subatomic particle motion. It's really the same thing Shirley was studying with bees in her mother's mason jars—particles of matter and their motion. Only now Shirley looks at tiny particles much smaller than an electron instead of bees. And she uses a computer instead of her eyes. But that is another story.

■　■　■

Follow-Up Activities

Young Shirley Jackson struggled to understand the basic building blocks of all substances and the patterns of matter and motion.

Here are some fun, easy, and powerful activities you can do to better understand the nature of the basic building blocks of matter and of basic observational physics.

Topics to Talk About

1. **Shirley Jackson's experiment.** Shirley Jackson looked at matter by looking at bees in a jar. Did she *have* to study bees, or could she have studied anything else? (*She could have looked at trees, weeds, birds, worms, buildings, or any other visible form of matter and still have studied the nature of and the patterns of matter. Shirley was also studying the link between matter and motion. She looked at the patterns of motion of the bees as well as the patterns of matter that made up the bees.*)

2. **Matter:** What is matter? (*Matter is the stuff, the substance, that makes up every physical object.*) How do you describe it? (*By the characteristics of the whole substance and of its building-block parts.*) When do you stop tearing it apart into smaller and smaller bits? (*When you can no longer tear it apart or see the new, smaller pieces.*)

3. **Building Blocks of Matter.** What are the major blocks of matter around you? (*The list probably includes walls, floors, clothes, people, windows, air, books, etc.*) What are the smallest building blocks of those different substances that you can see? (*This list probably includes grains, bits, fibers, flakes, specks, drops, and particles.*) Are there smaller common building blocks that are too small to see with a naked eye? (*Yes.*) What are they? (*The list includes cells, molecules, atoms and subatomic particles.*) What substances hold those building blocks in common? (*All matter is composed of these same basic building blocks.*) How can you detect and study them? (*With microscopes, electron microscopes, and other high-tech equipment.*)

4. **Patterns.** Look for patterns in the various levels of building blocks of the matter you discovered. (*Especially check brick walls, window placement and alignment, classroom doors in a hallway, hallway floor tiles, folds in window or stage curtains, and light fixtures.*) Did you find any? (*You should have found lots.*) Do the patterns and kinds of patterns appear again and again? (*Usually the same simple patterns appear over and over again.*) What are they?

From *Stepping Stones to Science.* © 1997 Kendall Haven. Teacher Ideas Press. (800) 237-6124.

Activities to Do

1. Necessary Equipment:

   - Paper and pencil for each student

   - One magnifying lens per group for the last experiment

   - Copies of "Student Worksheet," page 47

2. Building Blocks of Matter.

   - What are the major blocks of matter around you? Make a list of at least six you can easily see. Leave five or six lines between words on this list. The list probably includes walls, floors, clothes, people, windows, bookshelves, air, books, etc. Those are the basic building blocks of your school. The worksheet shows an example of such a list.

   - Can you see smaller building blocks that make up each of these big blocks of matter? What are the smallest building blocks of those different substances that you can see? Below the name of each major building block you have listed, and indented from it, list all the substances, the matter, and the smaller building blocks you can see that make up these bigger building blocks. Your list probably includes paint, putty, wood, glass, metal, nails, screws, chalkboard, etc.

   - Can you still see smaller bits, grains, flecks, drops, and particles of matter that make up these building blocks you have just listed? If so, list them beside the substance they make up on your paper.

   - Are there still smaller common building blocks of these bits of matter that are too small to see with a naked eye? How would you find and study these tiny particles?

   - Use a good magnifying glass to study the smallest particles you have listed on your paper. Can you now see even smaller particles that you couldn't distinguish before?

3. Patterns.

   - Look for patterns in the various levels of building blocks of the matter you discovered above. Readily apparent patterns show up in the bricks that make up brick walls, or in the individual window panes that make up a bank of windows. Also check the patterns of classroom doors in a hallway, hallway floor tiles, folds in window or stage curtains, light fixtures in the ceiling, and so on. Did you find many patterned building blocks of matter? Did the same patterns and kinds of patterns appear again and again? Did you see the same patterns appear in smaller and smaller bits of matter? What are they?

# STUDENT WORKSHEET
for Activities to Do
following a story about **Shirley Jackson**

1. The Building Blocks of Matter.

Major Building Blocks	Sub-Blocks	Sub-Sub-Blocks	Building Blocks Smaller Than the Eye Can See
Walls	Wood Paint Nails & Screws Chalkboard Door Glass Wallboard Plastic Light Switch Shelves	Grain, Splinters, Chips Flecks, Ridges	Individual fibers
Floor			
Windows			
Clothes			
Books			

Additional Reading

Good references in the children's library for further reading on matter and on Shirley Jackson's experiments include:

Berger, Melvin. *Solids, Liquids and Gasses.* New York: Putnam, 1989.

Clark, John. *Matter and Energy: Physics in Action.* New York: Oxford University Press, 1994.

Cobb, Vicki. *Why Can't You Unscramble an Egg?* New York: Lodestar Books, 1990.

Cooper, Chris. *Matter.* New York: Dorling Kindersley, 1992.

Darling, David. *From Glasses to Gasses.* New York: Dillon, 1992.

Friedhoffer, Robert. *Matter and Energy.* New York: F. Watts, 1992.

Hayden, Robert. *Seven African American Scientists.* Frederick, MD: Twenty-First Century Books, 1970.

Lapp, Ralph. *Matter.* New York: Time, 1973.

Lefkowitz, R. J. *Matter All Around You.* New York: Parents' Magazine Press, 1972.

Mebane, Robert. *Salts and Solids.* New York: Twenty-First Century Books, 1995.

Robinson, Fay. *Solid, Liquid or Gas?* Chicago: Childrens Press, 1995.

Time-Life Books, ed. *The Structure of Matter.* Alexandria, VA: Time-Life, 1992.

Consult your librarian for additional titles.

Physics

The "Gravity" of the Question

A Story of Isaac Newton's Discovery of Gravity in 1666

➤ A Point to Ponder

A pre-story question to focus student attention and interest on the story's central science theme—What would happen to you if there were no gravity? Would an apple still fall? What would happen to the Moon? What would happen to the Earth?

➤ Science Curriculum Links

This story deals with the physical science concept of gravity. What is gravity? How does it pull objects together? What creates the force of gravity?

Use this story to introduce a unit on planets and stars (their motion is controlled by gravity), as part of a unit on physics, or to introduce a famous and important scientist to your class.

➤ Key Picture-Maker Words

The following words create mental pictures important to the understanding of this story. However, not all your students may be familiar with each of them. Here are ways to quickly review these words and concepts to ensure that your students get the most out of these moments in science.

1. **Force:** A force is strength, energy, or power exerted or brought to bear against an object. Your muscles create force. Electricity creates force. Wind creates force. You must apply a force to an object to make it move or to deform the object.

    Lay a pencil on a table. One force, gravity, holds it to the table, trying to pull (move) it down to the center of the Earth. How many other forces can you find or create to move this pencil?

    Blow on it. The wind of your breath creates a force that can move the pencil. Push it with your finger, elbow, or nose. In each case your muscles are creating a force that moves the pencil.

Burning gasoline in an engine changes chemical force into mechanical force that can move a car and could move the pencil.

If an iron band were wrapped around the pencil, the magnetic force of a magnet could move it.

Grab the pencil (or a stick) in both hands and break it. You exerted a force that deformed the pencil.

These are all examples of common forces that we create and use every day. See if your students can list other forces that affect their lives.

2. **Attractive Force:** An attractive force draws one object toward another. Iron filings are attracted to a magnet by a magnetic attractive force. (This is an easy and dramatic attractive force to demonstrate.) Gravity is another kind of attractive force. It draws *any* two objects together.

3. **Gravity:** The attractive force that draws every object toward every other object is called *gravity*. Unfortunately, gravity is a very weak force. Unless one of the objects is large (like the Earth), gravity is so weak that it is hard to measure and demonstrate.

   Still, it is gravity that holds us to the Earth. Our common name for how strongly gravity pulls us toward the Earth is our *weight*.

   If there were no gravity we would have no weight. In space where objects are too far from the Earth to be affected by its gravity, things are weightless.

   The Moon is much smaller than the Earth, so the force of gravity is smaller on the Moon. You would weigh less on the Moon than you do on Earth.

   Jupiter is much bigger than the Earth. Thus, gravity on Jupiter is stronger than it is on Earth. You would weigh much more on Jupiter than you do here.

4. **Mathematics:** Mathematics is the study, or science, of numbers. Addition is part of math. So is division, subtraction, counting, fractions, algebra, etc. Any study of numbers is math.

The "Gravity" of the Question

It was a beautiful country garden. Bees buzzed between the rows of trees. Butterflies flitted back and forth above grassy lawns. In the midst of the garden a young man sat gloomily with his back against a thick apple tree. He looked as if a private rain cloud hovered over his head.

The 23-year-old man was teacher and scientist Isaac Newton. He had long blond hair and a small, thin body.

Newton's seven-year-old nephew, Joshua Marsh, a bundle of thick brown hair and questions, darted out through a patchwork of wildflowers. "Why are you sitting out here when everyone else is playing inside?"

Newton answered, "I'm thinking."

" 'Bout what?"

Newton sighed and pointed into the afternoon sky. "The Moon."

Joshua was instantly excited. "I like the Moon. Is there really a man living in it?"

Newton shook his head. "The real question, Josh, is why doesn't the Moon fall down to Earth?"

"Maybe it doesn't want to?" answered Joshua hopefully.

Newton laughed and re   out to scruff young Joshua's hair. "That's as good as any of my answers. For that matter, if the Earth revolves around the Sun—"

"What's *revolve*?" interrupted Joshua.

"Revolve means to move around something in a circle."

"You mean if I run around this tree I'm revolving?"

"Yes. If you ran in a circle, you'd be revolving around the tree." Newton shifted his back against the tree trunk to a more comfortable position. "Where was I? Oh, yes. Why doesn't the Earth fall down to the Sun?"

Joshua scrunched up his face. "That's a silly question! The Sun is *up*. How can we fall *down* to something that's *up*?"

"I am a scientist, Josh. My job is to ask questions."

From *Stepping Stones to Science*. © 1997 Kendall Haven. Teacher Ideas Press. (800) 237-6124.

They both heard the familiar "thunk" of an apple falling to the soft ground, and turned in time to see a second apple fall from an overhanging branch and bounce once before settling gently into the spring grass.

It was certainly not the first apple Isaac Newton had ever seen fall to the ground, nor was there anything unusual about its short fall. All that was different were the questions in Newton's mind when the apple fell.

The falling apple gave Newton an important new question. "The apple falls to Earth while the Moon doesn't. What's the difference between an apple and the Moon?"

"That's easy," said Joshua. "The Moon's big and yellow. The apple's small and red."

But like a nasty winter cold, the question wouldn't leave Newton's mind. "What's the difference between the Moon and an apple? The apple fell. So some force must have pulled it down to Earth. Why doesn't that happen to the Moon?"

Again he sighed. Questions, questions, questions.

As a steady rain fell that night, Newton paced across his room. Suddenly he stopped and stared out the window. The rain was *falling* to Earth, just like the apple.

What force made the rain fall? The same force that made the apple fall? Did some force make everything fall to Earth?

Questions, questions, questions.

Newton paced and thought. "Maybe there is a force that attracts every object to the Earth. But why should they only be drawn to the Earth? Maybe it's a great force that pulls, or attracts, every object to every other object—some universal attractive force. Things fall to Earth instead of each other because the Earth is so much larger. The bigger the object, the greater the pull of this force."

Newton began to tremble with the excitement of his discovery: a universal attractive force pulling every object toward every other object, its strength depending on the sizes of the two objects being attracted.

Then he collapsed sourly into a chair. His private rain cloud reformed over head. *Then why isn't the Moon pulled down to Earth? Why isn't the Earth pulled to the Sun? I still must be missing something. But what?*

Questions, questions, questions.

Next morning, Joshua was playing with a ball just behind the house. His ball was tied to a string held tight in his fist. He swung the ball, slowly at first, and then faster and faster until it stretched straight out on its string, whistling over Joshua's head. The two family dogs barked and leapt after it.

From his window, Newton was thunderstruck by an obvious answer. "A string holds the ball in. But its motion makes it want to fly off, to escape. There are *two* forces pulling on the ball, and also two forces pulling on the Moon—the universal attractive force pulling it toward Earth, and its motion pushing it away. It doesn't fall because they just balance each other. A ball on a string is just like the Moon circling the Earth!"

Newton dashed downstairs and burst out the back door. "Josh, I need your ball for an experiment." He snatched the ball and string out of his young nephew's hand.

"Hey! I'm playing with that."

"I'll give it right back, Josh. I just need it a second."

Newton spun the string. The faster the ball spun, the harder it pulled out on the string. He released the string. Joshua's ball soared across the lawn and landed in thick blackberry bushes.

"Hey! You lost it!"

"No, Josh. It *escaped*. And without the universal attractive force holding *it* in, the Moon would also escape into space."

"That's not the Moon. That's my ball, and I'm telling!"

Newton grabbed his nephew by the shoulders. "Don't you see?" he laughed. "The spinning ball wanted to fly off. But the pull of the string wouldn't let it. The spinning Moon also wants to fly off into space. But, just like a string, the pull of the universal attractive force won't let it."

Joshua looked confused. "There's a string attached to the Moon?"

"An invisible one," answered Newton. "The Moon *is* just like an apple. They are both pulled down to Earth, but the Moon's motion as it revolves around the Earth keeps it from falling. There are *two* forces pulling on the Moon, and we just discovered what they are."

"We did?" asked Joshua, looking longingly at the thorny blackberry bush. "What about my ball?"

With the joy of this answer bubbling in his mind, Newton turned for the house. "First, come with me."

From *Stepping Stones to Science.* © 1997 Kendall Haven. Teacher Ideas Press. (800) 237-6124.

He ran to his study and began to scribble complex mathematical equations in his journal. "What's that?" asked Joshua, pointing a finger at the page Newton was quickly filling.

"An answer this time instead of more questions, Josh."

"My ball gave you an answer?"

Newton reached out and lovingly mussed up his nephew's rich brown hair. "Your ball, the apple, the rain, each of them held the answer. But I couldn't see it because I was asking the wrong question. I wondered why the Moon doesn't fall. Wrong question. The Moon *does* fall toward Earth. But its motion also makes it want to fly off into space. Instead of doing either, the Moon falls *around* the Earth, just like the ball fell around my hand until I let it go. In the same way, the Earth is falling around the Sun."

Joshua looked more worried than confused. "The Earth is falling?"

Isaac Newton paused tapping his pen. "I think this force should be called 'gravitation.' It's from the Latin. As I recall it means 'to come together,' more or less. Yes. Gravity, the universal force that pulls all objects together, the one force that will explain how and why the Moon and planets act as they do."

Joshua pointed at his uncle's journal. "Is that gravity?"

"No, Josh, this is mathematics. Mathematics describes gravity. Your ball and the apple demonstrated it. My job was to discover the right question."

Joshua pouted. "I hope your next job is to get my ball back. . . ."

But of course that was another story.

■ ■ ■

Follow-Up Activities

Isaac Newton struggled to understand why things fall to Earth, the general nature of attraction, and why all heavenly bodies *don't* crash down into each other when apples and rain *do* crash down into the Earth.

Here are some fun, easy, and powerful activities you can do to better understand gravity and the way this universal attractive force operates in our lives.

Topics to Talk About

1. **Gravity:** What is gravity? (*Gravity is a force that attracts any two objects toward each other. It is created by the very existence of the matter in the objects.*) Put two rocks on the ground. If gravity attracts all objects to all other objects, why don't the two rocks slide or roll toward each other? (*Gravity is proportional to the mass of the two objects. Rocks are very, very small compared to Earth, so the force of gravity attracting them to each other is very small compared to the force pulling them down toward the Earth. Other, much larger forces overpower the attraction of gravity, including friction, drag, air resistance, and the gravitational pull of the Earth on the two rocks.*) How does gravity affect our daily lives? (*Gravity holds us and everything else in our world to the ground. It makes a car stay on the road, makes your breakfast cereal stay in the bowl and on the table, makes rain fall, makes water fall into the sink, and makes your bed stay put on the floor. Every aspect of our lives depends on gravity to keep us and the objects around us where we expect them to be.*)

2. **Overcoming Gravity:** Can you overpower gravity? (*Yes. You do it every time you stand, climb stairs, or jump.*) Why can't you escape into space? (*You jump by pushing off the ground. When in the air you have nothing to push against to create more upward force. Gravity pulls on you no matter where you are. Rockets use powerful motors to create upward force while they are in the air. Thus, they can escape Earth's gravity and travel into space.*) How does gravity pull on us? (*The pull of gravity decreases as the distance between the two objects increases. While flying in an airplane at 30,000 feet, you weigh less then you do standing on the ground. The distance between you and the Earth has increased, so gravitational pull [which we call our weight] has decreased.*)

3. **Understanding Gravity:** Why is gravity the same for every object? (*Gravity is a pull created by the Earth. The force of that pull is the same for every object on Earth. Put those same objects on another planet, or on the Moon, and the pull of gravity on them would be different. How it would be different depends on whether the new planet were bigger or smaller than the Earth.*) Without gravity, what would happen to the Moon and the Earth? (*Both would spin off into outer space. Gravity, the attractive force between the Sun and each of the planets, is the only force that keeps us in our orbit.*)

Activities to Do

1. Necessary Equipment:

    -   A narrow metal or plastic tube six to twelve inches long
    -   About three feet of string
    -   Small weights (several metal washers are ideal)
    -   A larger weight (for example, a small block of wood)
    -   A plastic tub (round dishpan-sized pan)
    -   A small plastic or metal bowl or pan with vertical sides
    -   A wooden stirring spoon
    -   Water
    -   Copies of "Student Worksheet," page 58

2. Overcoming Gravity.

    Are you stronger than gravity? Can you overpower gravity? Let's see if you can.

    -   While sitting, place a book on the floor in front of you. Now stand and pick up the book, holding it at shoulder height. Did you just overpower gravity?

    -   Yes, you did. Gravity pulled both you and the book down. You exerted a greater force and made both you and the book rise. You are stronger than gravity.

    -   Then, why can't you leap out into space and escape the Earth's gravity all together? You can only push upwards while you have something solid to push against. Gravity pulls you down no matter where you are. To escape into space you'd need a fifty-mile-high stairway to climb (so you'd always have something solid to push against). Of course, you'd probably get tired climbing half a million stairs!

3. Understanding Gravity—Making Your Own Moon.

    Isaac Newton discovered that two forces act on the Moon. Gravity pulls the Moon straight toward Earth. The motion of the Moon pulls it out into space. The net effect of these two balanced and opposing forces (one pulling the Moon toward Earth; one pulling the Moon away from Earth) is to make the moon forever fall *around* the Earth, instead of either toward or away from it.

    Newton was able to identify those two forces and develop the mathematical expressions to describe the way in which they acted on the Earth, the Moon, and on all other masses. Let's see if you can build a simple model representing the gravitational pull between Earth and Moon and see how the Moon's motion balances this powerful force.

    -   Insert a piece of string through your tube and tie the small washers or other small weight to one end. Tie the larger weight onto the string's other end. See the diagram on the worksheet.

- Hold the tube vertically in one hand. What happens? The heavy weight drops, pulling the string through the tube until your small weights crash into the top of the tube. This happens because gravity pulls down harder on the large weight, and no other force is acting to oppose gravity.

- Try the experiment again. This time start with the small weight and about six inches of string hanging out of the top of your tube. Again hold the tube vertically in one hand. Support the large weight in your other hand, holding it just below the tube.

- Twirl the tube in your hand so that the string and small weight spin straight out. The spinning weight will pull the string out farther and farther until most of the string is spinning like a helicopter blade out of the top of your tube.

- Gently let go of the large weight. What happens? If the large weight drags down the string and small weight, spin the small weight faster. You can spin the small weight fast enough to pull the large weight up to the bottom of the tube. Now the small weight can lift the larger weight. Do you know why?

- In this simple model, the large weight is like Earth. The small weight is like the Moon. Gravity tries to pull the Moon to Earth just as gravity pulled the small weight to the top of your tube. But when the small weight spins (just as the Moon spins around the Earth), its motion tries to pull it away to fly off into space.

- The Moon spins around the Earth. If it spun too fast, the force of its motion would pull it out into space. If it spun too slowly, the Earth's gravity would pull it crashing into us.

- Only when it maintains just the right speed do these two forces exactly balance each other and let the Moon fall around the Earth. These are the two forces Isaac Newton discovered. And your experiment just demonstrated how they work.

4. The "Other" Force—Centrifugal Force.

    The force of the Moon's motion that pulls it away from the Earth is called *centrifugal* force. Let's do another experiment to look at the power of centrifugal force.

    - Half fill a large tub with water. Then fill a much smaller bowl or pan with less than one inch of water. Float the bowl in your large tub as shown on the worksheet illustration. What happens to the water in the bowl? It just sits there, smooth and level, right? That is because no force other than gravity pulls on the bowl's water, and gravity pulls evenly down on every bit of that water.

    - Now give the bowl a twist, spinning it faster and faster by stirring it with a wooden spoon. As the bowl speeds up, what happens to the water inside? Now it climbs up the sides of the bowl, defying (or overpowering) gravity. The middle of the bowl should be dry.

    - What force makes the water do this? Centrifugal force. The spinning motion pulls the water out trying to fling it out across the room. This is the same force that keeps the Moon from crashing into the Earth. It is the force Newton discovered with his nephew's ball and string.

# STUDENT WORKSHEET
for Activities to Do
following a story about **Isaac Newton**

1. Overcoming Gravity.

        Can you? _____ Yes _____ No

2. Make Your Own Moon.

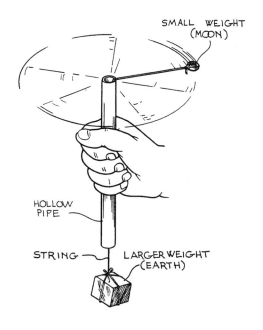

3. Centrifugal Force

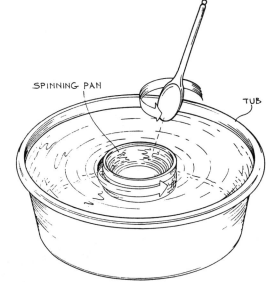

Additional Reading

Good references in the children's library for further reading on gravity and on Newton's experiments include:

Bixby, William. *The Universe of Galileo and Newton*. New York: American Heritage Publishing, 1974.

Branley, Franklyn. *Gravity Is a Mystery*. New York: Crowell, 1986.

Christeanson, Gale. *In the Presence of the Creator: Isaac Newton and His Times*. New York: Collier Macmillan, 1984.

Fauvel, John, ed. *Let Newton Be!* New York: Oxford University Press, 1988.

Haines, Gail. *Which Way Is Up?* New York: Atheneum, 1987.

Hall, A. Rupert. *Isaac Newton: Adventurer in Thought*. New York: Blackwell, 1992.

———. *Giants of Science*. New York: M. Cavendish, 1991.

Ipsen, D. C. *Isaac Newton, Reluctant Genius*. Hillside, NJ: Enslow, 1985.

Land, Barbara, and Myrick Land. *The Quest of Isaac Newton*. Garden City, NY: Garden City Books, 1960.

Lerner, Aaron. *Einstein and Newton*. New York: F. Watts, 1973.

Maury, Jean-Pierre. *Newton: The Father of Modern Astronomy*. New York: H. N. Abrams, 1992.

McTavish, Douglas. *Isaac Newton*. New York: Bookwright Press, 1990.

Narlikar, Jayant. *The Lighter Side of Gravity*. San Francisco, CA: W. H. Freeman, 1982.

Rattansi, M. *Isaac Newton and Gravity*. London: Priory Press, 1974.

Rocard, Jean Michelle. *Newton Versus Relativity*. New York: Vantage Press, 1992.

Sitweitka, Albert. *Physics: From Newton to the Big Bang*. New York: F. Watts, 1986.

Skurzynski, Gloria. *Zero Gravity*. New York: Bradbury Press, 1994.

Van Cleave, Janice. *Gravity*. New York: John Wiley, 1993.

Westfall, Richard. *Never at Rest*. Cambridge, England: Cambridge University Press, 1980.

Consult your librarian for additional titles.

Physics

"Teetering" at the Beginning of Knowledge

A Story of Archimedes' Discovery of the Lever in 259 BCE

➤ **A Point to Ponder**

A pre-story question to focus student attention and interest to the story's central science theme—What is a lever? Have you ever used one, or played on one? Where? What do levers do?

➤ **Science Curriculum Links**

This story deals with the physical science theme of mechanical machines. How do simple machines work? What is a lever, and how does a lever accomplish work?

Use this story to introduce the concepts of mechanics (how mechanical things work), levers, early scientists, or proportions.

➤ **Key Picture-Maker Words**

The following words create mental pictures important to the understanding of this story. However, not all your students may be familiar with each of them. Here are ways to quickly review these words and concepts to ensure that your students get the most out of these moments in science.

1. **Incline:** An incline is something that slants at an angle somewhere between horizontal (flat) and vertical (straight up).

   To demonstrate an incline, lay a ruler on a table. It is now flat, or horizontal. Lift one end of the ruler and rest it on a book (or short stack of books) with the other end still on the table. The ruler is now inclined.

   Have your students search the school for inclines. The railings on stairs are inclined. How many others can they find?

2. **Triangle:** A triangle is an area enclosed by three straight sides. Cut a piece of paper into a triangle to demonstrate this common shape. Have your students search for triangles in the places and objects they see around them.

3. **Triangular Prism:** A triangular prism is an elongated triangle. Each end is shaped like a triangle. The sides are inclined rectangles. The glass or plastic prisms used to separate light into a rainbow of color bands are usually triangular prisms.

   Bring a triangular prism into class both to fix its shape in your student's minds and to demonstrate a fulcrum and balance beam, using the prism and a ruler.

4. **Seesaw:** A seesaw is a long plank, balanced in the middle and used as a children's plaything. One child sits on one end. A second child sits on the other. As one child rocks up, the other rocks down. Many schools and public parks have playground seesaws.

5. **Fulcrum:** A fulcrum is the point around which a lever turns. A seesaw's fulcrum is the balance point in the middle of the seesaw.

   In this story, four boys drag a wood plank to a rock and swing the plank up and down as it balances on the rock. The rock is the fulcrum for that plank.

   Archimedes uses his sister's play blocks to do an experiment. He uses a triangular prism as a fulcrum for a short stick.

6. **"Three Times as Heavy":** Saying that one rock is three times as heavy as another is a way of comparing the weights of the two rocks. It says that it would take three of the small rocks to weigh as much as the one bigger rock.

   One of your students might be three times as heavy as a baby brother or sister. This says that it would take three babies to weigh as much as that one student.

   Bring in four rocks, three small and one approximately three times the size of each small rock. Use a triangular prism and ruler (balance beam) to show that the big rock balances three little rocks (that it is three times the weight of one of the little rocks).

"Teetering" at the Beginning of Knowledge

"Archimedes! Pay attention!"

Twenty-six-year-old Archimedes blushed and turned back to his teacher. "Sorry, Conon."

Above them, a fierce summer sun poured down its heat onto the island nation of Sicily. By our calendar the year was 259 BCE. Four men squatted under stubby olive trees for shade on a small knoll overlooking Syracuse harbor. One of the men, Conon, was a famous astronomy teacher. The other three were his students.

But Archimedes couldn't concentrate on astronomy. What fascinated Archimedes was a group of boys playing with a long piece of driftwood along the seashore. Laughing and dashing, they kicked up sprays of sand as they dragged the board to a waist-high rock. They slid the board along that rock until it exactly balanced, teetering gently up and down in the steady breeze off the choppy sea.

As seagulls circled over head, one boy straddled one end of the board while his three friends counted, "One, two, three!" and jumped hard onto the other. Squealing with delight, the lone boy was tossed into the air, crashing down to the sand with a soft thud and a cheer.

The boys slid the board along their balancing rock until one side was much longer than the other. The longer, heavier side dropped to the sand with a "thud." Giggling, three of the boys climbed up the slick, inclined board to sit on the short, top end. With the weight of three boys, the short end slowly swung down toward the beach. At the last moment the fourth boy jumped onto the rising long end, crashing it back to the sand, and flinging his three friends into the sky. All three squealed with glee as they landed on the board. Two laughed so hard they fell off.

Archimedes was fascinated! One boy had easily lifted three. Whereas before it had taken three to lift one. While the boys thought they were doing nothing but playing with an old, weather-beaten board, Archimedes thought he saw science at work. Exactly how did an old board make one boy strong enough to lift three friends?

"Archimedes!" snapped Conon. "Would you rather play on the beach like a child?"

The other students chuckled as Archimedes, face red with embarrassment, spun back to face Conon.

From *Stepping Stones to Science.* © 1997 Kendall Haven. Teacher Ideas Press. (800) 237-6124.

Archimedes asked, "Isn't it worthwhile science to ask how one weak boy is able to lift three friends by putting them on the end of a board that, itself, is already heavier than he can lift?"

"No!" snapped Conon. "Lifting is for servants and has nothing to do with science."

But Archimedes couldn't concentrate on astronomy. *I want to understand how that board gave one boy such strength*, he told himself as he walked home after class.

He would have to conduct experiments.

Archimedes grabbed five of his niece's play blocks: three cubes (two small, one larger), one rectangular block, and one triangular-shaped prism to act as the balancing point. He found a thin strip of wood to act as his lever. (Archimedes called his balancing board a *lever*, from the Latin word meaning "to lift.")

Archimedes placed the prism on a table and carefully balanced his lever across its point. His curling brown beard touched the table top as he picked up the two small cubes, one in each strong hand, and leaned close to watch. His blue eyes sparkled with excitement.

"Why are you playing with my blocks?" asked his six-year-old niece.

Startled, Archimedes snapped straight up, knocking his lever to the floor. "I'm not playing. This is a science experiment."

"*Looks* like you're playing," she insisted. "Can I play, too?"

"When you try to learn, it's an experiment," answered Archimedes.

"Please?" she begged. "They're *my* blocks."

"You can be my assistant," said Archimedes. "First, pick up my lever."

"Your *what*?" asked his niece.

"That piece of wood."

"Oh."

Again Archimedes placed the middle of his lever on the point of his niece's triangular prism. It balanced. On each end of this board he placed one of the small cubes. The whole thing balanced like two children on a seesaw, rocking slightly up and down.

From *Stepping Stones to Science.* © 1997 Kendall Haven. Teacher Ideas Press. (800) 237-6124.

Archimedes picked up the large cube to represent the weight of the extra two boys. He held it over one of the balanced cubes.

"When are we going to play something *fun*?" asked his niece.

"Shhh!" whispered Archimedes. "This is an experiment, and it *is* fun."

"No it isn't," she whined.

Archimedes dropped the large cube. It crashed down onto the lever, smashing that end to the table. The other end shot up. The small cube on it flew into the air, just as the lone boy had on the beach.

Archimedes' niece giggled. "I like *that*."

"What does this experiment teach me?" asked Archimedes, his forehead wrinkled in deep thought. "That when a greater weight, or force, pushes down on one end of a board, the heavier end goes down, and the lighter one rises. That's just what happened on the beach."

Archimedes smiled and clapped his hands. "Learning is such a wonderful thing! What did the boys do next? Oh, yes. They slid the board way over to one side so that one boy could lift three."

Archimedes slid his board across the point of his triangular block until most of it was on one end. The long, heavy end dropped to the table.

"It's getting boring again," complained his niece. "Let's bounce something else in the air."

"Shhh. This is an important part of our experiment."

Archimedes placed the large cube and one of the small cubes on the short end of his board. It was like balancing three boys on that end. The short end began to sink toward the table.

At the last second Archimedes dropped the last small cube on the rising, long end of his balance board. Crash! It dropped back to the table, flinging the other cubes into the air.

Archimedes' niece laughed and clapped her hands.

Archimedes stroked his beard and muttered, "And what does *this* experiment teach me?"

Then he cried out in joy and slapped the table so hard the blocks all jumped. "That's it!" he shouted.

His niece squealed, "You scared me!"

"But now I see how the board made one boy so strong." Like a light shining through the foggy dark of his mind, Archimedes saw simple proportions. "When a small weight pushes down on a long board, it creates as much force as a large weight pushing down on a short board. The force each weight creates is proportional to the lengths of board on its side of the balance point."

A boy could easily lift a stone 10 times his own weight—if he understood proportions and levers. He need only get a long board and have his side be 10 times as long as the side he wedged under the stone. Then when he sat on his own raised end, his side would come down, and the heavy stone would rise up!

His niece shook her head. "Maybe tomorrow you'll do an experiment that's *fun*."

Archimedes laughed and nodded. "But think how much we learn from experiments. In one afternoon I have learned how a lever lets people lift heavy weights, and that mathematics really describes how our world works in a very practical and useful way."

No human had tried to use science and mathematics to understand a simple physical occurrence in the world before. But curious Archimedes did. How he used that new understanding to create our very first scientific principles and concepts, however, is another story.

■　■　■

From *Stepping Stones to Science*. © 1997 Kendall Haven. Teacher Ideas Press. (800) 237-6124.

Follow-Up Activities

Archimedes struggled to understand two things: the nature of a common lever and the most basic relationship between science and the physical world around us.

Here are some fun, easy, and powerful activities you can do to better understand the principles governing the operation of a lever.

Topics to Talk About

1. **Balance:** What does it mean to "balance"? What do we mean when we say a person "balances" on a stool? When two weights exactly balance? (*We mean that the person falls neither one way nor the other; that neither of the two weights can pull the other one down toward the Earth. Really, what we mean is that the various* forces *acting on the person [or on the weights] exactly cancel each other out so that there is no net force acting on the body.*) What does balancing feel like? Have you ever balanced? What do forces have to do with balance? (*Balance is a static position when something doesn't move. Any time a force acts on a body, it creates movement. The only way a body can remain in balance—motionless—is for there to be no net force pushing on it. Because there are always forces pushing [or pulling] on a body [e.g., gravity], the forces must be equal and opposite so that the net effect of all forces is canceled out.*) When you balance on a stool, what forces have to balance? (*Gravity pulling down balances your muscles pushing up; gravity pulling you to one side [if you lean a little to one side] balances your muscles pulling you back the other way.*)

2. **The Relationship Between Length of Lever Arm and Force:** Have you ever used a lever to lift something? Is it easier to lift something when the lever arm on your side of the fulcrum is longer, or when it's shorter? (*Longer.*) Why? Could you make the lever arm on your side so short that you couldn't lift a one pound weight? (*Yes.*) What would that look like? Can you make a simple lever look like that?

3. **Proportions:** *Proportion* is the name of a mathematical term that compares two quantities. When we use a proportion we say, "Quantity #1 is to something as quantity #2 is to something else." We might say, "It's so cold in here that the temperature in this room is to the outside temperature as the freezer is to the refrigerator!" Have you ever used proportions? Have you ever seen them? What would they be good for?

Activities to Do

1. Necessary Equipment. Each group of students will need:

   - Small (8" to 12") light balance beam
   - Sturdy, pointed object to use as a fulcrum

- Series of small, uniform weights

- Two good rulers for measuring distances

- Copies of "Student Worksheet," page 68

Wooden paint stir rods (free at most paint stores) will do nicely for beams; Lego® building blocks or small batteries (9 volt, AA, or AAA) are examples of good weights.

2. Getting a "Balanced" View of Levers.

- In small groups, balance a balance beam over your fulcrum on a sturdy table. Think of a seesaw if you're having trouble envisioning what a balance beam looks like. Have a supply of equal-sized weights handy.

- Place equal weights (one block, one battery, etc.) on each end of your balance beam. Slowly slide the beam over your fulcrum until it exactly balances. That is, until the beam rests as nearly horizontal as you can make it.

- Compare the two sides, or lever arms, of your balance beam. Do they appear to be the same length? As accurately as you can, draw this balance and weight over the fulcrum on line #1 of the enclosed worksheet.

- What does this show you? It shows that two equal weights must be the same distance from the fulcrum if they are going to balance each other.

3. Piling It On.

- Now add a second weight to one end of the balance beam and rebalance. Again compare the length of the lever arm on each side of the fulcrum. Which side is longer? The side with one weight or the side with two weights? Draw your results on the worksheet in line #2.

- What does this show you? It shows that smaller weights need a longer lever arm in order to balance larger weights.

- Add a third weight to the heavy end and repeat the comparison. Now add a fourth weight. Draw each of your results on the worksheet as a way to compare each experiment.

- Keep adding weights and rebalancing until one side of the balance beam is so short you can no longer balance the lever.

- Did you see a pattern emerge from your comparisons? You should see that, as one weight grows larger, its lever arm has to grow shorter in order to keep the lever balanced. Does this sound like the simple proportions Archimedes discovered?

- Notice how a small weight, or force, can balance a large weight, or force, if it has a longer lever to push down on. On a seesaw, could you balance five people your same size? Where would you have to place them?

- If you wanted to balance a 50-pound weight and a 5-pound weight on a 10-foot board, could you guess where to place the fulcrum so the two sides would balance?

From *Stepping Stones to Science*. © 1997 Kendall Haven. Teacher Ideas Press. (800) 237-6124.

# STUDENT WORKSHEET
for Activities to Do
following a story about **Archimedes**

1. A Balanced View.

    Draw a picture of your balance beam and weights over the fulcrum points below each time you add a new weight and rebalance your beam.

    Example drawing:

2. Draw your balance beam with one weight on each side.

3. Draw your beam with one weight on one side and two weights on the other.

4. Draw your beam with one weight on one side and three weights on the other.

5. Draw your beam with one weight on one side and four weights on the other.

6. Draw your beam with one weight on one side and five weights on the other.

Additional Reading

Good references in the children's library for further reading on levers, on proportions, and on Archimedes' experiments include:

Allen, Pamela. *Mr. Archimedes.* Bath, NY: Lothrop, 1980.

Bendick, Jeanne. *Archimedes and the Door to Science.* New York: F. Watts, 1972.

Clagett, Marshall. *Great Science in Antiquity.* New York: Abeland-Schuman, 1965.

Dijkslerhuis, E. J. *Archimedes.* Princeton, NJ: Princeton University Press, 1987.

Gardner, Martin. *Archimedes, Mathematician and Inventor.* New York: Macmillan, 1965.

Harvey, Ted. *The Quest of Archimedes.* New York: Doubleday, 1972.

Hellman, Hal. *The Lever and the Pulley.* New York: Evers, 1971.

Ipsen, D. C. *Archimedes, Greatest Scientist of the Ancient World.* Hillside, NJ: Enslow, 1988.

Jonas, Arthur. *Archimedes and His Wonderful Discoveries.* Englewood Cliffs, NJ: Prentice-Hall, 1973.

Lafferty, Peter. *Archimedes.* New York: Bookwright, 1991.

Lampton, Christopher. *Seesaws, Nut Crackers, and Brooms.* Brookfield, CT: Millbrook Press, 1991.

Lexan, Joan. *Archimedes Takes a Bath.* New York: Crowell, 1969.

Sellers, Mick. *Wheels, Pulleys, and Levers.* Boston: Gloucester Press, 1993.

Wade, Harlan. *The Lever.* New York: Raintree, 1977.

Consult your librarian for additional titles.

Electricity

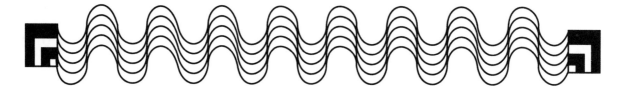

A "Spark" of Genius

A Story of Benjamin Franklin's Discovery of the
True Nature of Electricity in 1750

➤ A Point to Ponder

A pre-story question to focus student attention and interest on the story's central science theme—Is there any naturally occurring electricity in the world, or is all electricity manufactured at power stations? Is the electricity in a battery the same as the electricity in a house wall socket? Is all electricity dangerous?

➤ Science Curriculum Links

This story deals with the physical science theme of the nature of electricity. What is electricity? Is static electricity different than regular electricity? Is lightning different?

Use this story to introduce a unit on electricity, as part of a unit on famous Americans, or as part of a unit on inventors and inventions.

➤ Key Picture-Maker Words

The following words create mental pictures important to the understanding of this story. However, not all your students may be familiar with each of them. Here are ways to quickly review these words and concepts to ensure that your students get the most out of these moments in science.

1. **Leyden jar:** A Leyden jar is a large glass jar designed to collect electricity. Approximately the same height as a five-gallon water jug and roughly half the diameter, Leyden jars were partially filled with water, were lined with some metal foil, and featured a metal rod that extended up through a cork lid.

    When Leyden jars were first invented, scientists believed electricity was a liquid and thought they had to trap it in a jar, just as they would trap water.

2. **Spectacles:** When eyeglasses were first invented, they were called *spectacles*. That was the name everyone knew them by in 1750 when this story takes place.

3. **Static Electricity:** We have all felt static electricity, especially on days with low humidity. Your hair reaches up toward a brush and seems to stand straight out on its own. Static electricity has built up in your body and makes your hair do that.

   We have all felt a shock or spark jump from a metal doorknob to our hand. That is static electricity moving from your body to the door knob and back down into the ground.

   Take clothes out of the dryer at night with the lights off, and you'll see pops and sparks of light as you pull socks and shirts apart. Static electricity built up on the clothes as they tumbled in the dryer.

   Static electricity is an electrical charge that slowly builds up in a single, fixed place, such as your body or your socks in the dryer.

   Long before humans knew anything about other forms of electricity, they knew about and had felt static. It was Benjamin Franklin who named the stuff *electricity*. Before his experiments static electricity was called *static*, and lightning was called *lightning*. No one knew they were really two forms of one common energy source: electricity.

4. **Twine:** Twine is a heavy type of string where more than two strands are twisted together to form a stronger, thicker line. Twine, then, is thicker and stronger than string, but thinner and weaker than rope.

   While twine is not a good conductor of electricity, strong electrical charges can trickle along twine. This is what happened in Franklin's famous kite experiment.

A "Spark" of Genius

It started with an invitation to a turkey dinner two days before Christmas at the home of Mr. Benjamin Franklin. Six of his friends and neighbors were invited. I received one of those invitations since I, Simon Colfax, was *both* friend and neighbor to the great inventor.

Franklin, the 44-year-old statesman, publisher, and inventor, greeted us at the door with a sly giggle and a twinkle in his eye that said some gimmick, some new invention, was afoot. "Come in, come in!" he cried, whacking us merrily on the back and whisking us toward the kitchen. We stomped our feet and rubbed our arms to shed the outside winter cold.

William Mercer sniffed the air with a nose as sharp and demanding as his personality. "I smell no turkey dinner roasting."

"All in good time," laughed Franklin.

On Franklin's kitchen table we saw not the grand winter feast we'd been promised, but only two large Leyden jars.

Of course, we were familiar with Leyden jars. Static electricity was a very popular plaything in America in 1750. People would shuffle across a rug and reach out for a metal doorknob to get a spark, a sharp "pop!" and the thrill of a quick jolt running through a finger while everyone else laughed and cheered.

Leyden jars gave the same effect, only better. Invented just four years earlier by Professor Leyden, a Leyden jar was a large glass jar partially filled with water and wrapped with tinfoil around the outside. A metal rod extended up through a top cork to a round metal knob. Once a Leyden jar was charged with a hand crank, anyone who grabbed the knob while touching the tinfoil or other metal got a resounding shock while their hair stood on end. It was a wonderful party game!

But Franklin's Leyden jars looked different. They were coated both inside and out with foil. They were large, very large. And they were hooked together by a copper wire.

Franklin seemed very pleased as we gawked at the differences in his jars.

"This is no turkey dinner," grumbled William Mercer. "I came to eat, not play with static electricity."

"No, no! Don't touch," Franklin cautioned. "I have found a way to pack more power into my jars. Oh, it's all just basic science, really. But these jars now carry enough power to be dangerous, as you shall see."

He brought out a large and very live turkey, and said it was to be our dinner. To our amazement, Franklin said his Leyden jars packed enough electrical punch to kill the bird *and* spark the fire that would cook it.

William Mercer muttered, "I wish you had done that part this morning. Then you could tell us about it *while we ate* this afternoon!"

With turkey held tight under one arm, Benjamin began to describe his experiments with Leyden jars. Nothing pleased Benjamin more than to talk about his inventions. Soon his words excitedly ran together as he described this amazing electricity and the useful work it could do. His free hand gestured wildly this way and that through the air.

Carried away by his own enthusiasm, Franklin reached out one hand and laid it on the nearest Leyden jar.

There was a sharp crack, and a sizzling blue arc leapt from the jar to Franklin's fingers. He shot back half a dozen feet and crashed to the floor, dropping the turkey, which now ran wildly about the room, squawking. Dazed, Franklin slowly sat up, rubbed his eyes, and adjusted his spectacles. Then his face lit with the glow of discovery.

"That was exactly like a lightning bolt," Franklin repeated over and over again. "Exactly like lightning."

In 1750 everyone believed there were two kinds of electricity: safe static electricity that we could play with, and the fiery electricity that leapt from clouds as lightning. Franklin was the first to think that they might be the same.

We never got our turkey dinner that night. The Leyden jars were now drained of energy. Benjamin Franklin was lost to us, deep in thought about this new discovery. Was there really only one kind of electricity? How could he design an experiment to see if the electricity in clouds was the same as playful static?

He decided that the best way to show that all electricity was the same, whether explosive lightning or playful static, was to build a big Leyden jar to capture electricity which flowed from the clouds just as it did into the jars on his table.

Franklin's "Leyden jar for the clouds" would look different than the ones on his table but would have the same parts. He hooked a sharp metal wire onto a kite (to gather electricity from the clouds), then tied the kite to a long twine string. Electricity, he hoped, would slowly trickle down the twine to a large iron key tied to the bottom (which would act as a place to hold the electrical energy). The other end of the key was tied to a ribbon through which electricity could not flow. Electricity would be trapped in the key, just like it was in a Leyden jar. Franklin would hold the ribbon and thus be safe during the experiment.

What he needed now was a good thunderstorm.

When an afternoon storm brewed up dark and threatening a few weeks later, Franklin rushed to launch his kite. Wind howled, and the clouds boiled above us. A cold rain pounded down about our upturned collars. Twice I had to hold Franklin down as a fierce gust of wind grabbed hold of the kite and tried to rip it from his hands. The kite twisted and tore at the air like a rampaging bull. Our coats snapped in the howling wind, spraying rainwater like fountains. We could barely hear each other shout over the screeching gale.

Then it happened. No, a lightning bolt did not strike the kite, as has often been reported. And a good thing, too. A French scientist was killed a few months later by a lightning strike when he tried to repeat Franklin's experiment. No, what happened that stormy afternoon was that the twine kite string began to glow a faint blue. The fibers on the twine bristled straight out. We could almost see electricity trickling down the twine.

We stared at the key, waiting to see if it would also glow. But the key showed no evidence of the electricity building up inside it.

Franklin reached out a cautious finger closer and closer to the key. And pop! A spark leapt to his knuckle and shocked him—just like from his Leyden jar.

Franklin's son was along with us. He reached out a hand and a blue arc sizzled from key to finger. It made him cry out with fright, and he leapt back behind his father, shaking his hand.

The electricity in clouds, which everyone called lightning, really was the same as static electricity. There was only one kind of electricity. It was all the same. Franklin's experiment proved it.

Satisfied, Franklin reeled in the now-tattered kite, and we hurried inside for congratulations, hot cider, and a careful review and discussion of the experiment. Although it would take men like Michael Faraday of England and Samuel Morse of America another 50 years to fully understand the nature of electricity, Benjamin Franklin, on that stormy afternoon, led the world of science in a great step forward. But the struggles of Faraday and Morse are another story.

■ ■ ■

Follow-Up Activities

Benjamin Franklin struggled to understand the true nature of electricity, something he couldn't see or directly measure. He had to rely on observations of the effect of electricity to try to uncover its true nature.

Here are some fun, easy, and powerful activities you can do to better understand static electricity and the nature of electricity in general.

Topics to Talk About

1. **Electricity:** What is electricity? (*An energy source made up of moving electrons.*) Where do we find electricity? (*In nature as static electricity, as lightning, and in some animals, as with the electric eel. Otherwise, electricity is human-made, and we find it in power lines, wall sockets, and batteries.*) How do we use it? List all the times you use electricity in a day. What do we use it for? Is it dangerous? (*Yes, very dangerous. That is why every person working with or experimenting with electricity must protect themselves. Rubber is a good and common protector from electric shock because electricity can't flow through rubber. Notice that electric cords are all rubber-coated.*)

2. **Static Electricity:** What is static electricity and how is it collected? (*Static is a naturally occurring electric charge that builds up from friction. As two surfaces rub against each other, electrons are actually ripped out of molecules on one surface and attached to the other. As more and more electrons are pulled away, the surfaces build up an electric charge. We call it static.*) What determines how much static you can build up in your body? (*Atmospheric conditions—temperature and humidity—and the nature of the two surfaces being rubbed against each other.*)

3. **Safety with Electricity:** Which forms of electricity are least dangerous? (*Low-voltage, low-current electricity, such as static, or small batteries, such as watch batteries.*) Which are most dangerous? (*High-voltage, high-current power lines; large batteries; and lightning.*) How can you minimize your own risk when experimenting with electricity? (*Avoid direct contact with flowing electric current. Wear rubber gloves and shoes. Install circuit breakers in all electric lines. Make sure all electric equipment is properly grounded.*) Was Benjamin Franklin acting safely with his kite experiment? (*Actually, no. He wasn't protected from powerful lightning strikes. His only excuse was that no one knew the danger when he conducted his experiment. Now we know much better.*)

Activities to Do

1. Necessary Equipment. Your class will need:

    *   Three kinds of shoes: non-rubber-soled street shoes, rubber-soled tennis shoes, and sandals.

    *   Several common objects to test for static buildup. These can include a balloon, a sweater, a washcloth, a hand-sized block of wood, etc.

    *   Four squares of floor surfaces. Many schools have carpet squares for young children to sit on. Search these for different kinds and lengths of fibers. Use linoleum, hard wood, wool, and nylon if you can. Indoor-outdoor carpet can be an alternate if one of these types is unavailable.

    *   Copies of "Student Worksheet," page 78

2. Getting a "Charge" out of Static.

    Everyone has built up a static charge shuffling across a rug and gotten a small spark when it discharged from a finger to a metal doorknob. Everyone has heard the snap of static sparks when pulling off a sweater on a dry day. Many have done this in the dark and have seen the sparks.

    Did you know that those brief flashes of sweater sparks often hold as much as 20,000 volts of electric potential? While they have such a high voltage, or energy potential, they have only tiny electric currents. This keeps them from being dangerous. Compare that to household current, which is only 110 to 120 volts but has a much larger current flow and is very dangerous.

    Let's see if some surfaces build stronger static charges than others.

    *   Pick one metal object about waist height, preferably grounded, to act as the discharge point for your human static charge. Line up the four floor coverings next to it.

    *   The "results" you get from these tests will only be a sense of whether the spark created in each test was "big" or "small," whether it was "strong" or "weak," and whether it jumped a "long" distance or a "short" distance. None of the sparks you generate, for example, will jump much over one-quarter of an inch.

    *   Pick four students, each wearing a different type of shoes: street shoes, tennis shoes, sandals, and bare feet. They will each test each of the floor coverings. They must always shuffle, or rub their feet, across each floor sample the same way and for the same length of time. This way, any differences they detect in static sparks will come from differences in the floor coverings and shoe type.

    *   Testers shouldn't step off the floor covering they are testing until after they have reached out to discharge their static spark. They must slowly ease their finger closer to the chosen metal object (a doorknob, for example). Going very slowly allows them to tell the exact moment of discharge.

- Have several students watch to see whether the spark was "big," "medium," or "small"; and whether it jumped a "short" distance, a "medium" distance, or a "long" distance. The person who carried the spark will have to decide how "strong" or "weak" it felt. Record your results for each type of floor covering and shoe on the enclosed worksheet.

- Did patterns emerge? Did certain types of floor covering, or combinations of floor covering and foot covering produce consistently stronger or weaker sparks? Why do you think?

3. Time to Shuffle.

- Next, see if the length of time you shuffle affects the static charge you build up. For this experiment, use only the two floor coverings that produced the best sparks during your first experiment. Also, use only the two types of foot covering that produced the best sparks for those two floor coverings. Now retest these combinations to see what effect the length of time you shuffle back and forth to build up a static charge has on the apparent size of the resulting spark.

- Being sure to shuffle back and forth in exactly the same way each time, vary the length of time you shuffle your feet to build up a static charge. Try times of 5, 10, 20, 40, and 90 seconds. Could you tell if the spark grew stronger as shuffle time increased? Did the charge reach a peak level after some length of shuffling, so that more shuffling didn't produce additional static buildup? Use the worksheet to record your results for each of these four tests.

- All of the above tests were conducted on one day with one certain level of humidity, or water content, in the air. You can find the daily humidity in the newspaper or on TV weather reports. Wait for another day with a different humidity level and repeat the above static experiments. Try the experiments on one very humid day and on one very dry day.

- Could you see or feel differences in static charges between the two days? Why? See if you can find answers in your library.

# STUDENT WORKSHEET
for Activities to Do
following a story about **Benjamin Franklin**

1. Getting a "Charge" Out of Static.

   For each combination of foot covering and floor covering record your best estimate of spark size (big, medium, small), spark strength (strong or weak), and the distance it jumped from finger to metal.

	Street Shoes	Tennis Shoes	Sandals	Bare Feet
Hardwood				
Linoleum				
Wool Carpet				
Nylon Carpet				

2. "Time" for Static.

		1	2	3	4
Time of Shuffle	Floor Cover: _____ Shoe: _____	_____	_____	_____	_____
5 Seconds					
10 Seconds					
20 Seconds					
40 Seconds					
90 Seconds					

Additional Reading

Good references in the children's library for further reading on electricity and on Benjamin Franklin's experiments include:

Alder, David. *Benjamin Franklin: Printer, Inventor, and Statesman.* New York: Holiday House, 1992.

Aliki. *The Many Lives of Benjamin Franklin.* New York: Simon & Schuster Books for Young Readers, 1985.

Asimov, Isaac. *The Kite That Won the Revolution.* New York: Houghton Mifflin, 1973.

————. *How Did We Find Out About Electricity?* New York: Walker, 1973.

Clark, Ronald. *Benjamin Franklin: A Bibliography.* New York: Random House, 1983.

Daugherty, Charles. *Benjamin Franklin: Scientist & Diplomat.* New York: Macmillan, 1965.

Daugherty, James. *Poor Richard.* New York: Viking Press, 1961.

Davidson, Margaret. *The Story of Benjamin Franklin: Amazing American.* New York: Dell, 1988.

Draper, John. *The Life of Franklin.* Washington, DC: Library of Congress, 1977.

Fleming, Thomas. *The Man Who Dared the Lightning.* New York: William Morrow, 1971.

Franklin, Benjamin. *The Autobiography of Benjamin Franklin.* New York: Harper, 1964.

Meltzer, Milton. *Benjamin Franklin: The New American.* New York: F. Watts, 1988.

Osborne, Mary. *The Many Lives of Benjamin Franklin.* New York: Dial Books for Young Readers, 1990.

Potter, Robert. *Benjamin Franklin.* Englewood Cliffs, NJ: Silver Burdett, 1991.

Randall, Willard. *A Little Revenge: Benjamin Franklin and His Son.* Boston: Little, Brown, 1984.

Sandak, Cass. *Benjamin Franklin.* New York: F. Watts, 1986.

Stein, R. *Benjamin Franklin: Inventor, Statesman, and Patriot.* New York: Rand McNally, 1972.

Stewart, Gail. *Benjamin Franklin.* San Diego, CA: Lucent Books, 1992.

Stone, A. *Turned On: A Look at Electricity.* New York: Prentice-Hall, 1970.

Tamarin, Alfred. *Benjamin Franklin: An Autobiographical Portrait.* New York: Macmillan, 1969.

Tanford, Charles. *Benjamin Franklin Stilled the Waves.* Durham, NC: Duke University Press, 1989.

Tourtellot, Arthur. *Benjamin Franklin: The Shaping of Genius.* New York: Chelsea House, 1990.

Whyman, Kathryn. *Sparks to Power Stations.* Boston: Gloucester Press, 1989.

Wilson, M. *American Science and Invention.* New York: Bonanza, 1960.

Wright, Esmond. *Franklin of Philadelphia.* Cambridge, MA: Belknap Press, 1986.

Consult your librarian for additional titles.

Chemistry

The "Smell" of Success

A Story of Charles Goodyear's Invention of
Vulcanized Rubber in 1837-1839

➤ **A Point to Ponder**

A pre-story question to focus student attention and interest on the story's central science theme)—How many things have you used in the past week that were made of rubber? Are you wearing any rubber right now? What about shoes and elastic waistbands? Is all the rubber you've seen this week the same? What makes one kind of rubber different from another? What makes it change?

➤ **Science Curriculum Links**

This story deals with the physical science concept of change, especially chemical change. How does a substance change when other substances are added? What causes the change? How can we observe this change? How does heat or cold affect (change) a substance? Does boiling or roasting change a substance? Why?

Use this story as an introduction to the study of chemistry or to the nature of change through chemical combination, or as part of a unit on famous inventions.

➤ **Key Picture-Maker Words**

The following words create mental pictures important to the understanding of this story. However, not all your students may be familiar with each of them. Here are ways to quickly review these words and concepts to ensure that your students get the most out of these moments in science.

1. **Experiment:** An experiment is a test, trial, or procedure carried out under controlled conditions in order to discover some unknown value, effect, concept, or law.

    We all regularly conduct informal experiments, or tests. When your students were still babies they experimented with how to stand and walk. Their first attempts, or experiments, on how to control and direct their leg and body muscles and mimic the walking motion of their parents always failed. They collapsed back to the floor. From each failed experiment they learned more about what would and wouldn't work, until one experimental try finally succeeded.

An experiment is *any* planned test carried out while trying to discover something. Have your students try to think of other experiments they have conducted and other trial-and-error learning they have undertaken, even though at the time they didn't know they were conducting experiments. (Writing, reading, and riding a bicycle are all examples of what could be experiments.)

2. **Ingredient:** An ingredient is one element or component of a mixture. We use this word most commonly when we cook. Every recipe lists the ingredients that go into the dish being made and the amount of each ingredient.

Other mixtures and compounds have ingredients. The concrete that sidewalks, house foundations, and some roads are made of has four ingredients: sand, gravel, cement, and water.

Your breakfast cereal has ingredients: the cereal, milk, and maybe fruit on top. Each of these "ingredients" is also made up of other ingredients. Every mixture, or combination, is made up of ingredients.

3. **Mixture:** Stir two or more ingredients together. If those ingredients give up their old properties and combine into a new substance with different properties, it is called a *compound*. However, if those ingredients do not combine but stay in their original form with their original properties, it is a *mixture*.

Stir several spoonfuls of sand into a glass of water. The sand slowly swirls to the bottom, forming a thick layer of sand below with clear water above. The sand is still sand. The water is still water. The combination of the two is a mixture.

Now stir several spoonfuls of sugar into a glass of water. The sugar dissolves and disappears. It has merged with the water to form a new substance. This is a compound.

In this story Charles Goodyear says he is creating a "mixture" of five or six ingredients to create more useful rubber. Do you think he creates a mixture, or does he really create a compound?

4. **Magnesium:** Magnesium is a silvery metal found in the earth, in seawater, and in plants. It is an essential trace nutrient for all humans. It is used in metal alloys to provide extra strength and durability.

Charles Goodyear added magnesium to his rubber mixture to add strength and durability to his rubber clothes.

5. **Sulfur:** Sulfur is an abundant, nonmetallic element in the earth. Pure sulfur has a deep yellow color. It is used in gunpowder. It is part of the coating that makes matches burn. It is also a common ingredient in fertilizers.

   Sulfur is also a main element in the awful rotten egg smell everyone hates. If you have ever been near a volcano, you have probably smelled the stinky sulfur gas and steam hissing out of vents in the volcano's sides.

   Sulfur acts as a base (the opposite of an acid). Charles Goodyear added sulfur to his rubber to keep mild acids from destroying his rubber clothes.

6. **Turpentine:** Turpentine is used as a cleaning solvent to wash off oil-based paints. In stores, turpentine is often sold as "paint thinner."

   Turpentine comes from the essential oils distilled from coniferous and pine trees.

7. **Acid:** Acids are sour-tasting liquids (or water-soluble solids). Strong acids will badly burn your skin and are dangerous. We eat many mild acids. Fruit juices are acids (lemon juice, grapefruit juice, etc.). Vinegar (used in salad dressings and marinades) is an acid.

   However, stronger acids (such as battery acid or laboratory acids) are extremely dangerous and will dissolve almost anything they touch. They not only burn and dissolve substances, they can rip electrons and whole atoms out of molecules to form new compounds.

   The opposite of an acid is a base. Many household cleaners are strong bases. Water is in the middle between acids and bases. There is even a special scale, called the pH scale, to measure how acidic or basic any substance is. Low numbers on that scale are acids. High numbers are bases. Water, with a pH value of 7, is exactly in the middle.

   In this story, vinegar (a mild acid) dissolves Goodyear's rubber. A chemist friend suggests adding sulfur, a base, to Goodyear's rubber to protect it from the effects of acids.

8. **Dissolve:** We often use the word *dissolve* to mean to melt or to end. Near the end of *The Wizard of Oz* Dorothy splashes water on an evil witch and she dissolves, or melts away.

   When used to describe a chemical process, *dissolve* means to make something pass from a solid into a solution. Salt or sugar stirred into water dissolves in the water. Sand will not dissolve in water. Cocoa powder dissolves in warm milk to make hot chocolate.

   Have your students be on the lookout for things they see dissolve.

9. **Wood Stove and Firebox:** Modern American stoves are heated by natural gas or electricity. But neither of these sources of energy were available in the home until well after 1900. Before that, stoves were heated by burning wood.

   The front of a wood-burning stove normally had two doors. One larger one opened into the oven for baking food. A slightly smaller one opened to the firebox, or the place where wood was burned to create heat. A vent pipe had to lead from the firebox to the roof to lead the fire's smoke up and out of the house.

   In this story, Charles Goodyear uses a wood stove first to boil his rubber mixtures, and later to roast the rubber by pitching it directly into the firebox.

10. **Dry Ice:** Water (H_2O) exists in our normal world as a solid, a liquid, and a gas. Water is our name for the liquid form. Ice is our name for the frozen, or solid, form of water. Water vapor is what we call gaseous water. Another common chemical substance is carbon dioxide, CO_2, the gas we exhale each time we breathe.

    CO_2 is common as a gas, but, outside of the laboratory, never exists as a liquid. It can, however, exist as a solid. Solid CO_2 is called *dry ice* and is used as a refrigerant—most commonly for ice cream in ice cream trucks and in some retail stores.

    Dry ice has two advantages over regular ice: it is colder, and so keeps the ice cream harder and more frozen than regular ice would, and it doesn't melt. Dry ice changes from a solid (ice) not to a liquid (as with water) but straight to a gas. If you have seen dry ice, you have seen a white vapor, like a wispy cloud, rising from it. This vapor is CO_2.

11. **Lime:** Most people think a lime is a small, green, sour fruit, like a lemon. The fruit is one kind of lime. "Lime" is also the name of a dangerous chemical that can burn your skin and clothes as do strong acids. Lime, primarily a compound of calcium and oxygen, is used in many industrial and agricultural processes. Charles Goodyear got the idea to add lime to his rubber from local industrial plants that used it to strengthen various products.

The "Smell" of Success

"*Mother*! Father's doing it again!" yelled seven-year-old Charles Jr. from the hallway.

"Mommy! Daddy's making the house stink!" cried four-year-old Carol, holding her nose on the bare living room floor.

"I'm hungry!" complained five-year-old William, not wanting to be left out.

Susan Goodyear shook her head in frustration. "Charles?" she called to her husband, "I thought we agreed you wouldn't experiment with that awful-smelling rubber until you find a job and can support your family."

Charles Goodyear poked his head out the kitchen doorway. "But *this* experiment will work. I know it will!"

"You've said that about each of your last hundred experiments," Susan answered. She raised her eyebrows and tightened her lips. "Charles, you were supposed to buy groceries. Did you buy rubber instead?"

Nervously Charles fingered the hem of his shabby coat. "I got some groceries, Susan. I bought the rubber with the money that was left over."

"There hasn't been any 'left over' money in this house for five years!" Susan snapped. She was normally a very patient woman. But this was 1837. Five years of smelly rubber experiments and no income to support the family had pushed her to the limits of her patience.

"I'm *sure* I've figured it out this time," announced Charles, fanning the summer heat away from his face. "A nice man at the leather shop showed me how they turn cow hides into leather. They boil them in lime water. So I thought, 'if it works for leather, why not for rubber?'"

"It smells stinky!" whined all three children.

Susan glared at her husband. "Charles, you promised."

"But Susan," begged Charles. "Each experiment leads me closer to making rubber useful. First I added magnesium—"

"What's magnesium?" asked Charles Jr.

"Probably something else that stinks," said Caroline.

"Magnesium is a metal," corrected their father. "You can't smell it at all. Magnesium makes iron stronger. So I thought it might make rubber stronger, too. But now I think that before magnesium can work, I have to cook my

---

rubber in lime water just like leather. When this experiment works, I'll have invented reliable rubber clothes! Then we'll be rich and have all we want."

Charles Jr. slouched in the hallway. "All I want is to stop smelling burnt rubber."

"Our house always stinks," agreed Caroline.

Again feeling left out, William added, "I'm hungry!"

Rubber was well known by the nineteenth century. Columbus found children playing with it on his second voyage to the New World. Spanish explorers smeared thick coats of the milky-white sap of wild rubber trees on their clothes for waterproofing. An Englishman, Joseph Priestly, discovered in 1770 that rubber gum rubbed out his writing mistakes. He was the one who named the stuff "rubber."

Charles Goodyear believed rubber could have more important uses. But his dream of creating practical rubber clothes to protect his family had turned into a family nightmare.

First, Charles lost his job because he spent more time experimenting with rubber than he did minding his store. The family had to sell their furniture, good clothes, toys, and books to buy food.

The problem was that summer heat turned rubber into a sticky goo more like syrup. Winter freezes made rubber brittle so that it cracked and broke. To make rubber useful, Goodyear had to find a way to make it soft and, well, rubbery, but still strong and solid, at all common temperatures.

Charles ducked back into the kitchen to finish his experiment: a mixture of rubber, turpentine, magnesium, and his newest ingredient, lime. Charles boiled the thick black goo for half an hour while the children complained and held their noses. Then he let it cool and rolled the spongy blob into a thin sheet with his wife's rolling pin.

Would his new rubber stand up to heat and cold? Charles laid the rubber sheet on the back porch where the blazing summer sun could blast down on it.

Then he waited.

"Hey, Dad," called Charles Jr. "This rubber hasn't melted like all the others."

Boiling rubber with lime helped it withstand heat.

The family watched as Charles laid the rubber on a block of bitter cold dry ice. Again they waited.

From *Stepping Stones to Science*. © 1997 Kendall Haven. Teacher Ideas Press. (800) 237-6124.

Carol snatched up the rubber sheet and crumpled it between her hands. "Daddy, it doesn't crackle and pop like the other ones!"

Both Charles's and Susan's eyes lit with hope and excitement. The rubber stayed soft and rubbery, even when cold. It worked!

Three weeks later, in early September of 1837, the doors of "Goodyear's Rubber Clothes Shop" opened to a crowd of buyers, newspaper reporters, and onlookers. Sales were brisk. The cash drawer filled. Everyone wanted wearable rubber clothes.

For three days the Goodyear family was happy.

Then the first coat was returned with a large, goopy hole drooping down one side. "A few tiny drops of vinegar splashed on it," announced the angry woman. "I will not pay for a coat that disintegrates when a drop of salad dressing touches it!"

Charles was shocked. "Vinegar did *that* to my rubber? Oh, no!"

By week's end almost every coat, shoe, and pair of pants had angrily been brought back for a refund. Any acid dissolved Charles' rubber to a puddle of goo. The family was once again penniless.

"But . . . but that experiment was *so* close," pleaded Charles. "I know I'll find the right way to make rubber useful with just one more experiment."

"No more experiments!" insisted his wife.

"No more stinky smell!" demanded Charles Jr. and Carol.

"I'm hungry," added little William.

One morning in early February 1839, while his wife was out shopping and the children were playing with friends, Charles sneaked into the kitchen for a new experiment. He had a new ingredient to add to his rubber mix: sulfur. A chemist friend said that sulfur might protect rubber from acids. Charles decided he should add sulfur to his rubber.

Charles mixed rubber, turpentine, magnesium, lime, and sulfur into a baseball-sized black blob. He was just heating a pot of water to boil the goo when he saw his wife strolling up the front walk.

Oh, no! Charles couldn't let Susan see his experiment. She'd be furious, and he'd never get to find out if his new idea worked. In desperation he pitched the blob into the firebox of their hot wood stove to hide it. The rubber sizzled as he slammed the firebox shut and turned to greet his wife.

Susan's eyebrows arched suspiciously as she sniffed the air. "It smells like rubber in here. . . ."

From *Stepping Stones to Science*. © 1997 Kendall Haven. Teacher Ideas Press. (800) 237-6124.

Charles sheepishly lied, "Oh, it must be that *old* batch I was looking at earlier. . . ."

Susan stepped outside to fetch the children. Charles snatched his charred mess from the family stove. It hadn't hardened into a solid rock. It was still soft and rubbery.

"Interesting," muttered Charles.

He grabbed the rubbery mass with both hands and pulled hard. It stretched out and then snapped back to its original shape as soon as he let it go. "Very interesting!" Charles shouted.

Charles Jr. was the first of the children back in the house. With an ear-to-ear grin, Charles giggled, "Pull it, son."

Charles Jr. stretched the rubber and let go. SNAP! The rubber flew back into its original shape. "Wow, Dad! Your rubber never did *that* before."

"What is this?" demanded Susan, standing angrily at the door. "A rubber experiment?"

"I did it!" answered Charles, joy in his voice. "This experiment works!"

By the end of the day Charles had tested his burned rubber with heat and cold. It passed both tests easily. He sprinkled vinegar and other chemicals on his new burned rubber. It survived without a mark. He gave his burned rubber every test he could think of. It always worked!

Sulfur and dry heat. Those were the final two ingredients Charles had searched so hard to find. He had to add sulfur and burn the mixture instead of boiling to create useful rubber. Charles named the process "vulcanization" after the Roman god of fire, Vulcan.

Vulcanized rubber is one of the most important and versatile products of our modern world. From rubber bands to rain boots to tires, we use vulcanized rubber every day.

However, Charles and his family saw neither wealth nor fame from his discovery. After suffering through years of smelly kitchens and hardship to reach his discovery, Goodyear and his wife died poor and unknown, just as they had lived. But that's another story.

■ ■ ■

Follow-Up Activities

Charles Goodyear struggled to understand a process of chemical change. He had a base product, rubber, that had great potential and also great problems. He sought out other substances that had properties he wanted to add to his rubber and then experimented for a way to combine them.

Here are some fun, easy, and powerful activities you can do to better understand the concept of chemical combination and resulting change in the properties of a substance.

Topics to Talk About

1. **Properties of a Substance:** How do we describe a substance and its properties? (*We first describe physical properties our senses can detect—look, smell, feel, taste, etc. Next we describe a substance by its useful or unique properties. Finally, we describe a substance by the way it interacts with other common substances [e.g.: Is it water soluble or not?].*) How do we discover what the properties of a substance are? (*By observation and experimentation.*)

2. **Changes by Mixture:** What makes the properties of a substance change? (*Change happens either when the physical conditions affecting that substance change [temperature goes up or down, humidity increases or decreases, atmospheric pressure changes, etc.], or when the substance is combined with other substances to form a new substance combining the characteristics of the original two.*) How do we find out how some mixtures of substances will change the substance's properties? (*By observation and experimentation. Try some new combination and see what happens. If the experimenting scientist has experience with the substances being combined, the results of such a chemical combination can often be predicted.*)

Activities to Do

1. Necessary Equipment:

   - One glass jar (pint size is good)

   - One raw egg

   - White vinegar (about one pint)

   - One cup of milk

   - A tablespoon

   - Copies of "Student Worksheet," page 92

From *Stepping Stones to Science.* © 1997 Kendall Haven. Teacher Ideas Press. (800) 237-6124.

2. Is Rubber Rubber?

    • Is all the rubber you use and see the same? Does it all look alike and act alike? For one day keep a detailed list of every bit of rubber you see or use. Use the worksheet to list the use of the rubber and the physical characteristics of that particular piece of rubber—thickness, color, elasticity, hardness, springiness, etc.

    • By the end of a day you probably will have created quite a long list. Rubber is all around us in our modern world. More interesting, you probably noticed that the properties of rubber changed a lot from one use to another. Rubber for tires is very different than rubber in rubber bands. Rubber on your shoes is different than hard rubber bumpers or soft foam rubber padding.

    • Different substances have been added to base rubber to create each of these different types of rubber. They are all rubber. But their different properties come from the different substances added to the basic rubber mix.

3. Changing a Substance—The Acid Test.

    Charles Goodyear discovered that even mild acid changed the physical properties of his rubber clothes. Let's do an experiment and see how mild acids can chemically change the physical properties of a substance.

    • Pour half a cup of milk into a glass jar. Add three tablespoons of common white vinegar and stir briefly. Allow the jar to sit for two to three minutes.

    • What happened to the milk? Have you ever heard the poem about Little Miss Muffet who sat on a tuffet eating her curds and whey? You just separated the milk into curds (the solid part) and whey (the watery liquid part).

    • Why did this change occur? Vinegar is a mild acid. The acid chemically changed the milk, causing it to physically change. You added a chemical that physically changed the original substance—just as acid changed Charles Goodyear's rubber.

    • Goodyear added sulfur to his rubber to prevent acid from destroying his rubber clothes. See if you can also protect milk from separating when you add acid vinegar. Carefully pour three tablespoons of household ammonia into a second half cup of milk before you again add three tablespoons of vinegar.

    • What happened this time? Ammonia prevented vinegar from changing the milk, just as Goodyear's sulfur prevented vinegar from dissolving his rubber clothes. Remember. This jar of milk is still ruined. Do not drink it! Pour it down the drain.

4. Testing a Good Egg.

Let's try another experiment to see how a chemical change changes the physical properties of a substance. Again we will use vinegar, a mild acid, to create this change. Vinegar is the same kind of acid that destroyed Charles Goodyear's first batch of rubber clothes.

- Place a raw egg in a glass jar. Be careful not to crack the egg. Cover your egg with common white vinegar and cover the jar's opening.

- Watch what happens inside. Bubbles form on the eggshell's surface and slowly increase over the hours. Within a day the eggshell will have disappeared, and a thin membrane will have formed around the egg in its place.

- What happened? The acid in vinegar chemically reacted with the calcium in the egg's shell. This reaction caused carbon dioxide bubbles to form and the calcium to change form, combining with the acid to create a clear liquid compound.

- Again, a chemical change altered the physical properties of an original substance. While Charles Goodyear had a specific goal in mind for each chemical he added to his rubber mixture, the process of his experiments was still the same as the ones you have just completed.

From *Stepping Stones to Science*. © 1997 Kendall Haven. Teacher Ideas Press. (800) 237-6124.

# STUDENT WORKSHEET
for Activities to Do
following a story about **Charles Goodyear**

1. Listing the Rubber.

   Make a list of every product you use in one day that contains rubber; list the specific use of the rubber; and describe the physical properties of that rubber.

PRODUCT	USE OF RUBBER	PROPERTIES OF RUBBER

Additional Reading

Good references in the children's library for further reading on rubber, on chemical compounding, and on Charles Goodyear's experiments include:

Asimov, Isaac. *Asimov on Chemistry.* Garden City, NY: Doubleday, 1974.

Basmajian, Ronald. *Through the Molecular Maze.* Merced, CA: Bioventures, 1990.

Beeler, Nelson, and Franklyn Branley. *Experiments in Chemistry.* New York: Crowell, 1972.

Buehr, Walter. *Rubber: Natural and Synthetic.* New York: Morrow, 1974.

Cobb, Vicki. *Gobs of Goo.* New York: Lippincott, 1983.

———. *Chemically Alive.* New York: Lippincott, 1985.

Collier, Richard. *The River That God Forgot: The Story of the Amazon Rubber Boom.* New York: Dutton, 1988.

Cooper, Elizabeth. *Discovering Chemistry.* New York: Harcourt Brace, 1979.

Cossner, Sharron. *Rubber.* New York: Walker, 1986.

Freeman, Mae. *Fun with Chemistry.* New York: Random House, 1972.

Haines, Gail. *What Makes a Lemon Sour?* New York: Morrow, 1977.

Lewington, Anna. *Antonio's Rain Forest.* Minneapolis, MN: Carolrhoda Books, 1993.

Mebane, Robert, and Thomas Rybolt. *Adventures with Atoms and Molecules.* Springfield, NJ: Enslow, 1995.

Mitgutsch, Ali. *From Rubber Tree to Tire.* Minneapolis, MN: Carolrhoda Books, 1986.

Morgan, Alfred. *First Chemistry Book for Boys and Girls.* New York: Scribner's, 1977.

Morgan, Nina. *Chemistry in Action.* New York: Oxford University Press, 1995.

Quackenbush, Robert. *Oh, What an Awful Mess!* Englewood Cliffs, NJ: Prentice-Hall, 1980.

Snyder, Carl. *The Extraordinary Chemistry of Ordinary Things.* New York: John Wiley, 1992.

Stone, Harris, and Bertram Siegel. *The Chemistry of Soap.* Englewood Cliffs, NJ: Prentice-Hall, 1978.

Time-Life Books, ed. *The Structure of Matter.* Alexandria, VA: Time-Life, 1992.

Whyman, Kathryn. *Chemical Changes.* New York: Gloucester Press, 1986.

Zubrowski, Bernie. *Messing Around with Baking Chemistry.* Boston: Little, Brown, 1981.

Consult your librarian for additional titles.

Chemistry

"Funny" Rubber

A Story of James Wright's Invention of Silly Putty in 1944

➤ **A Point to Ponder**

A pre-story question to focus student attention and interest on the story's central science theme—How many things can you make Silly Putty do? Would you call it a scientific discovery? Would you call it a toy? Or would you call it both?

➤ **Science Curriculum Links**

This story deals with the physical science concepts of chemistry, chemical compounds, and chemical experiments, and with the process of invention.

Use this story to introduce chemical science, for a unit on invention and technology, or as a prime example of the process of chemical scientific experimentation.

➤ **Key Picture-Maker Words**

The following words create mental pictures important to the understanding of this story. However, not all your students may be familiar with each of them. Here are ways to quickly review these words and concepts to ensure that your students get the most out of these moments in science.

1. **Artificial and Synthetic:** Natural rubber from a rubber tree *is* rubber. Something human-made that acts like rubber and looks like rubber is *artificial* rubber. If that artificial rubber were created by chemically combining elements and substances, it is called *synthetic* rubber.

   Have your students search for artificial and synthetic products. Many fibers used to make clothes are synthetic. In department stores they can find "synthetic" listed on the labels of many garments.

   Artificial grass is used in many stadiums. Especially when set up outdoors, human-made lighting is called "artificial" lighting. How many other examples can your students find?

2. **Silicone:** Silicon is a basic element, one of the most abundant elements in the Earth's crust. Silicon*e* refers to chemical compounds made with silicon. You can most often find silicone in oils and lubricant sprays in hardware stores (or in the family workshop).

   Silicone also is the base ingredient for an excellent synthetic rubber. That artificial rubber was discovered late in World War II by the same GE research group talked about in this story. First James Wright invented Silly Putty. Then other team members developed synthetic silicone rubber.

3. **Acid (Boric Acid):** Acids are sour-tasting liquids (or water-soluble solids). Strong acids will badly burn your skin and are dangerous. We eat many mild acids. Fruit juices are acids (lemon juice, grapefruit juice, etc.). Vinegar (used in salad dressings and marinades) is an acid.

   However, stronger acids (such as battery acid or laboratory acids) are extremely dangerous and will dissolve almost anything they touch. They not only burn and dissolve substances, they can rip electrons and whole atoms out of molecules to form new compounds.

   James Wright combined one kind of acid, boric acid, with silicone, hoping to create a new, synthetic, rubber-like compound. What he created instead was Silly Putty.

   The opposite of an acid is a base. Most household cleaners are strong bases and can be just as dangerous as strong acids.

4. **Chemistry:** Physics is the study of matter and energy and the relationship between the two in any substance. Chemistry is the study of the structure (composition) of a substance and of the changes that happen to a substance.

   Chemists ask questions like, "What happens when two substances are mixed?" "What happens if they are heated or cooled?" and "What affects the properties of a substance?"

"Funny" Rubber

As it did every workday morning, the half-filled green company bus squeaked to a stop at the guarded Gate Number 3, the worker's entrance to the sprawling General Electric Research Laboratory. The bus door swung open with a rush of hot air from the early summer winds, and a uniformed guard entered to check ID badges. ID checks were designed to make sure only employees could enter the lab grounds. The guard slowly walked down the bus aisle, comparing each ID picture with the faces before him. Many of those faces still yawned over morning papers and coffee.

The guard stepped back off the bus and waved at a second security man in the guard shack. "They're all okay."

The guard shack man nodded and pulled a lever. The outer gate swung open, and the bus inched forward past security dogs and armed guards to a second fence. Once the outer gate closed tightly behind the bus, an inner gate swung open, and, as it did every workday, the bus pulled into the top-secret research plant with part of the day shift and research crew.

This was the spring of 1944. World War II was in full swing. This plant was dedicated to critical War Department research. As the bus came to its second stop, James Wright, a chemist, rose from his seat and started down the aisle.

"See you tonight, Jim," called a neighbor and fellow researcher, waving. James Wright waved back and stepped into the blowing heat in front of Building 242, a two-story, thick-walled cement building. Everyone inside was working on a War Department project to invent human-made, or artificial, rubber. James Wright, like many of the other chemists working with him, had been working on this one project for more than three years.

So far the project had failed. Both War Department generals and top General Electric managers had begun to demand that these scientists "produce something, and fast!"

James Wright joined the line of fellow researchers marching through the main Building 242 entrance and past yet another security guard. Finally inside the cozy lab he shared with two other chemists, James plopped down into his desk chair next to an overflowing sand box just inside their lab door.

Rubber was needed for truck tires, boots, airplane tires, and a host of other war-related uses. The demand was far greater than the available supply. These researchers had the job of finding a cheap source of artificial or synthetic rubber. James's group was studying sand as a possible source for that synthetic rubber.

From *Stepping Stones to Science*. © 1997 Kendall Haven. Teacher Ideas Press. (800) 237-6124.

Actually, they were searching for a way to make a rubber substitute from silicon. But silicon makes up a big part of what we call sand. If their project worked, there was certainly plenty of sand, and thus, plenty of silicon for artificial rubber.

"What are you working on this week, Ernst?" asked James as he rose from his desk and slipped on a white lab coat.

"High-temperature silicone alloys," replied Ernst Gretcher, already heating a test tube over his gas burner. "What about you?"

"I'm just finishing the silicone-acid tests," said James. Adjusting goggles and long rubber gloves, he stepped to a small work area next to the lab sink. From a high shelf he pulled down a series of tall bottles, each labeled with the name of a different acid and partly filled with clear liquid.

He poured a small amount of silicone oil into each of a long row of clear glass dishes. Then he opened his lab journal and wrote notes to describe this day's setup.

John McCuthy, the third chemist working in the lab, walked in sipping coffee from a heavy paper cup. "Finding anything?"

"Just starting!" called both James and Ernst without looking up from their work.

"Keep at it," said John, settling into his own work area with a deep sigh. "The Army is screaming for artificial rubber NOW."

The first of James's tests scheduled for that day was to try mixing silicone oil with boric acid. One by one he counted and released a dozen drops of boric acid onto the silicone oil in the first dish. The mixture bubbled softly around the edges. Thin wisps of white smoke rose from the dish. The mixture turned cloudy and jelled into a spongy blob as the reaction stopped.

James reached out with a glass rod and poked the soft, lumpy goo. It felt springy—like rubber. He tried several chemical tests to see if the goo was dangerous or unstable. No. It seemed harmless and, more importantly, rubbery.

James picked up the gooey mass. It held together and didn't seem to stick to his gloves. He set it back on the counter and pressed down on it with his thumb. The goo slowly oozed out on all sides. He picked it up and lightly threw it down onto the lab counter. It bounced. Not well, but it bounced.

From *Stepping Stones to Science*. © 1997 Kendall Haven. Teacher Ideas Press. (800) 237-6124.

Excitement and hope began to grow. Maybe this stuff would work as artificial rubber. James called, "Ernst, John, come and look at this."

Both men peered over James's shoulder at the soft goo in his hand.

"Try to stretch it," said Ernst.

"Try to smash it," demanded John.

James gripped the goo with both hands and slowly pulled. The goo stretched way out like saltwater taffy. But it didn't spring back at all. That was bad. Rubber was supposed to spring back.

He placed the goo on a counter and smashed it with a hammer. The goop shattered into a dozen fragments. Hopes were shattered along with this funny goo. Rubber wasn't supposed to shatter.

The stuff reformed into a single gooey blob as soon as James rolled the individual pieces back together into a ball. But it didn't matter. James's goo had failed the rubber test. No, it wasn't a rubber substitute.

Ernst and John shrugged and returned to their own experiments.

James hesitated, rolling the ball of whatever-it-was between his fingers. It wasn't rubber, but it was . . . well, fun.

Feeling suddenly mischievous, James tossed the goo at Ernst and both men laughed. Ernst bounced it to John. The goo ball bounced off a table and hit John on the chin. All three men laughed.

John pretended to be a basketball player and tried to bank the ball off one wall and into a bucket next to their sand box. He missed and the ball rolled across James's sport coat, which lay on his desk.

"Hey look, the goo picks up lint!" exclaimed James and all three laughed even harder.

Word spread through Building 242 of the strange blob James Wright had created. All morning a constant trickle of engineers and scientists flowed into the lab to take a look.

"Go ahead. Bounce it. Now smash it with a hammer!" Each new person put James's goo through its ever-expanding series of tricks. "Now smoosh it out on the Sunday newspaper comics. Now peel it back up. Look! It even picks up Little Orphan Annie." And everybody laughed all over again.

At 2:00 that afternoon Dr. William Grayling, the group director, stormed into the lab with an awful scowl on his face. "I hear you've been playing instead of working in here all day."

"Oh, no, sir!" answered James. "We've been working."

Dr. Grayling frowned. "I keep hearing about some goo that makes people laugh."

James's cheeks flushed red with embarrassment. "That's silicone oil mixed with boric acid, sir. It was one of my experiments."

"Is it a possible rubber substitute?" demanded Dr. Grayling.

"No, sir. It isn't. It's not strong enough, and it won't spring back when you stretch it. But let me show you what it *can* do."

"NO!" Dr. Grayling slammed his fist on Wright's desk. "I have to file a report on today's progress in three hours. I do not want to have to say my group spent the entire day playing with some silly toy. Now back to work!"

Over the next few days James Wright's silly goo was slowly forgotten. More than two dozen brilliant engineers and scientists had tested and examined the stuff. But no one was able to see a practical use for it. Eventually even James filed it away and forgot it.

Five years later, in 1949, young Peter Hodgson, who had been a student lab assistant in Building 242 during the war, finally saw the practical use no one else had recognized. Dr. Grayling had been exactly right. It *was* a silly toy. Hodgson made a large batch of James Wright's goo, packaged it in plastic Easter eggs, and named it "Silly Putty." Within two years it became the most popular toy in the Western world. But that's another story.

■ ■ ■

Follow-Up Activities

James Wright struggled to understand the chemical structure of rubber and to create synthetic rubber. That is, he struggled to find chemical elements he could combine to create a substance that had the same physical properties as rubber.

Here are some fun, easy, and powerful activities you can do to better understand the processes of chemical combination and chemical creation.

Topics to Talk About

1. **Serious Science:** Does science always have to be serious? (*No. Science is a systematic, thorough exploration into the unknown. At times it can be funny or even silly and still be careful, good science.*) Have you ever worked on something that was funny but was also a serious project?

2. **Synthetic or Natural:** What is the difference between synthetic and natural substances? (*Natural substances occur in or are produced by nature or natural processes. Synthetic substances are human-made and produced by the synthesis, or combination of, two or more other substances.*) Could you find all natural substances if you went searching through the world? (*Not necessarily. Some natural substances might now be extinct, or gone from the Earth. Others could be buried deep within the Earth and not available on or near the surface.*)

3. **What to Combine:** If you were trying to create a new synthetic substance, how would you decide which chemicals and original substances to add to your new combination? (*If you knew chemical reactions, you could try to anticipate the chemical reactions that would occur when two substances were combined. Otherwise, you would have to look for substances with physical and chemical properties you wanted in your new substance, and add those to the mix.*)

Activities to Do

1. Necessary Equipment:
   - Two small glass jars, one of which should have a lid
   - A one-liter plastic soda bottle
   - White vinegar (about one pint)
   - Steel wool
   - Baking soda (one teaspoon)
   - Household ammonia (one tablespoon)
   - A tablespoon
   - One large (15" to 18") balloon
   - Copies of "Student Worksheet," page 102

From *Stepping Stones to Science*. © 1997 Kendall Haven. Teacher Ideas Press. (800) 237-6124.

2. Your Very Own Green Blob.

    James Wright created a brownish blob (Silly Putty) during his chemical experiments with silicone. Let's see if you can chemically create your own green blob.

    - Half fill a glass jar that has a lid with steel wool. Add enough vinegar to cover the steel wool and screw on the lid. Label this jar "Iron Acetate," because that is the name of the chemical compound you are creating inside the jar.

    - Set the jar aside for four to five days.

    - Now pour two tablespoons of this iron acetate into a second glass jar. Add two tablespoons of household ammonia and stir.

    - What happened? Record your results on the worksheet. A green, jelly-like substance should have been created. Where did it come from?

    - Iron in steel wool combined with vinegar acid forms iron acetate. A chemical reaction occurs as soon as this liquid mixes with cleaning ammonia (actually ammonium hydroxide). In this reaction, the original compounds break apart and reform into two new substances.

    - In other words, iron acetate plus ammonium hydroxide produces ammonium acetate plus iron hydroxide.

    - Notice that nothing new was created. There was only an exchange of material. Originally you had iron, acetate, ammonium, and hydroxide. At the end you still have these four substances. But they have been rearranged into new combinations. The original two substances were clear liquids. Now they make a green, jelly-like blob. That is the nature of chemical combination. And that is exactly what James Wright tried to do with silicone to produce synthetic rubber.

3. The Form of Matter.

    Let's do one more experiment to see how the physical form of substances can be changed by simple chemical combination.

    - Pour one tablespoon of baking soda into a plastic soda bottle. Pour five tablespoons of vinegar into a large balloon. Attach the open end of this balloon over the mouth of the bottle. Tape the balloon onto the bottle with ordinary cellophane tape.

    - Raise the balloon, allowing vinegar to pour into the bottle and mix with the baking soda.

    - What happened? Again record your results on the worksheet. The mixture should begin to bubble and the balloon inflate.

    - You started with a liquid acid (vinegar) and a solid base (baking soda). When they chemically combine, they change into new substances. One of these is water, and one is carbon dioxide gas. That harmless gas is what inflated the balloon.

    - Again, no new elements were created. New substances were formed when the original elements were recombined by chemical action from their old substances into new ones. These are the kinds of experiments chemists like James Wright do all the time.

# STUDENT WORKSHEET
for Activities to Do
following a story about **James Wright**

---

1. Making the Green Blob.

   A. Steel Wool + Vinegar = Iron Acetate

   B. Iron Acetate + Ammonium Hydroxide = ??

   Record what happened when you mixed these two clear liquids: _____

   _____

   _____

   _____

2. Blowing Up a Balloon.

   Record what happened when you mixed baking soda and vinegar: _____

   _____

   _____

   _____

Additional Reading

Good references in the children's library for further reading on chemical experiments, on Silly Putty, and on Wright's experiments include:

Asimov, Isaac. *Asimov on Chemistry*. Garden City, NY: Doubleday, 1974.

Basmajian, Ronald. *Through the Molecular Maze*. Merced, CA: Bioventures, 1990.

Beeler, Nelson, and Franklyn Branley. *Experiments in Chemistry*. New York: Crowell, 1972.

Buehr, Walter. *Rubber: Natural and Synthetic*. New York: Morrow, 1974.

Cobb, Vicki. *Gobs of Goo*. New York: Lippincott, 1983.

———. *Chemically Alive*. New York: Lippincott, 1985.

Collier, Richard. *The River That God Forgot: The Story of the Amazon Rubber Boom*. New York: Dutton, 1988.

Cooper, Elizabeth. *Discovering Chemistry*. New York: Harcourt Brace, 1979.

Cossner, Sharron. *Rubber*. New York: Walker Publishers, 1986.

Freeman, Mae. *Fun with Chemistry*. New York: Random House, 1972.

Haines, Gail. *What Makes a Lemon Sour?* New York: Morrow, 1977.

Jones, Charlotte. *Mistakes That Worked*. New York: Doubleday, 1985.

Lewington, Anna. *Antonio's Rain Forest*. Minneapolis, MN: Carolrhoda Books, 1993.

Mebane, Robert, and Thomas Rybolt. *Adventures with Atoms and Molecules*. Springfield, NJ: Enslow, 1995.

Mitgutsch, Ali. *From Rubber Tree to Tire*. Minneapolis, MN: Carolrhoda Books, 1986.

Morgan, Alfred. *First Chemistry Book for Boys and Girls*. New York: Scribner's, 1977.

Morgan, Nina. *Chemistry in Action*. New York: Oxford University Press, 1995.

Snyder, Carl. *The Extraordinary Chemistry of Ordinary Things*. New York: Wiley, 1992.

Stone, Harris, and Bertram Siegel. *The Chemistry of Soap*. Englewood Cliffs, NJ: Prentice-Hall, 1978.

Time-Life Books, ed. *The Structure of Matter*. Alexandria, VA: Time-Life, 1992.

Whyman, Kathryn. *Chemical Changes*. New York: Gloucester Press, 1986.

Zubrowski, Bernie. *Messing Around with Baking Chemistry*. Boston: Little, Brown, 1981.

Consult your librarian for additional titles.

Biological Sciences

The "Evolution" of a Voyage

*A Story of Charles Darwin's Discovery of His Theory
of the Evolution of Species in 1835*

➤ **A Point to Ponder**

A pre-story question to focus student attention and interest on the story's central science theme—Do species stay the same over time? If not, why do they evolve, or change? What makes a species change? When a species changes, how does it manage to make itself change?

➤ **Science Curriculum Links**

This story deals with the biological science concepts of diversity, evolution, and adaptation. Do species evolve and adapt over time? Do they change to better fit their surroundings? How could such a theory be tested and proved?

Use this story to enliven the scientist Charles Darwin, to introduce the concepts of evolution and adaptation, as an example of the scientific process as applied to biological field studies, or as part of a unit on birds and their characteristics.

➤ **Key Picture-Maker Words**

The following words create mental pictures important to the understanding of this story. However, not all your students may be familiar with each of them. Here are ways to quickly review these words and concepts to ensure that your students get the most out of these moments in science.

1. **Voyage:** Voyage is another word for *travel*, used most often when that travel is by ship and across the ocean. We wouldn't say, "I'm going to voyage to grandmother's house." We'd say, "I'm going to travel to grandmother's." But Christopher Columbus set out on a voyage across the Atlantic. The *Titanic* set out on a voyage. When you hear "voyage," think "ocean travel by ship."

2. **Galapagos Islands:** The Galapagos Islands sit 600 miles off the west coast of Ecuador, South America, in the Pacific Ocean. They are an important research spot because they are some of the newest islands on Earth. That is, the volcanic eruptions that formed the islands happened fairly recently. By studying how life develops on these new islands, scientists get a peek at how life might have originally developed on the much older land masses of the world.

3. **Lava:** The fire deep inside volcanoes is hot enough to melt rock. When a volcano erupts, red-hot liquid rock flows out across the earth, burning and destroying everything it touches. As this rock cools, it hardens and darkens into black, new rock. The boiling, liquid rock and hardened black rock are both called "lava."

   Sometimes lava hardens smooth and looks like black pudding poured across the land. Sometimes it hardens crinkly and rough like cinders. Either way, it is lava.

   Most of the rocks and mountains you see on Earth are many millions of years old. Lava is special because it is brand new rock. There are places in Hawaii where volcanoes are erupting right now and where all the rock and all the plants you can see are younger than you are!

4. **Finch:** Finches are a general group of small songbirds, found almost worldwide. Sparrows and goldfinches are common American finches. Finches are numerous in England, so Darwin was familiar with them. Almost all finches in the world eat seeds.

   Finches became important to Darwin's understanding of the process of evolution because the finches he found on the Galapagos Islands ate nuts and berries instead of seeds and had different-shaped beaks—beaks much better suited to eating berries or nuts.

5. **Evolution (Evolve):** Evolution is the process of changing over long periods of time. Projects evolve over time as the people doing them discover better ways to do what they have to do. Towns and cities evolve over time as new people and companies move in and old ones move out, as buildings age and are abandoned, and as new ones are built to replace the old.

   Species also evolve, changing over time to make it easier for them to survive. Until Charles Darwin discovered this kind of evolution, everyone thought that all species always had been, and always would be, exactly the way they were.

6. **Adapt:** We all want to adapt to our surroundings, to fit in. If you went to a new school, you'd want to fit in with the children in your new class, to get along, and be like them.

    Plants and animals act the same. When they find themselves in a new area, a new environment, they want to fit in. How do they do it? They *adapt* to their new surroundings, just like you would. The need to adapt is the main driving force behind evolution, or change, for all species.

7. **Environment:** Your environment is the things and conditions around you. This includes the weather, the climate, the plants, the animals, the land, and others of your own kind.

    Your environment is another word meaning "all the things that make up where you are."

The "Evolution" of a Voyage

The shrill chirping of a thousand bright yellow birds echoed in my ears. I ran back to the ship as fast as I could, stumbling through twisted fields of crunchy black lava. Ragged waves of lava, looking like a sea of thick, black pudding, rose and twisted before me. My path was blocked by wide cracks, and by pockets where dense steam and stinging yellow vapor hissed from deep in the rock. The broken lava was covered by patches of stunted, sunburnt brush that looked more dead than alive.

Though I had been told they would not harm me, I still circled wide around the groups of shiny black lizards that seemed to love this frightful land. At times over a hundred of them slithered across each other, all three to four feet long with pink, flickering tongues that seemed as long as their tails. They scurried out of my way on stubby legs, hissing fiercely, as I ran past.

My name is Jason Crum, and, until signing on as assistant mate for this voyage in 1833, I had lived all my 22 years in green, pleasant England. Then I sailed off on the HMS *Beagle* to see the world. If I had known the world was going to look like this, I'd have stayed at home.

"Mr. Darwin! Mr. Darwin!" I called as soon as I spotted the ship's scientist, 28-year-old Charles Darwin studying one of the brittle scrub trees. I thought he should see the birds I had found.

Darwin looked up and saw me wave. "Did you find something, Jason?" he called back.

Panting to catch my breath, I nodded. "I think so, Mr. Darwin."

"Either you did, or you didn't, Jason. Now which is it?" Mr. Darwin studied me with his dark eyes that always seemed to frown under thick, bushy eyebrows. His eyes even frowned when he laughed, which he rarely did—mostly, I think, because he was always seasick, even after three years at sea.

"I think I found a new kind of finch," I answered. "But their beaks are different than any finches we've seen before. So I'm not positive that's what they are." Finches are a common bird in England. We had found them on several other islands on this voyage. But the finches here were, well, different.

"Really?" he exclaimed. "*Another* new finch? Show me where, Jason."

This was our second day investigating James Island, the fourth of the Galapagos Islands for us to explore. It was already late October 1835. But here, right on the equator in the Pacific Ocean, no day or season seemed any different than any other.

Mr. Darwin lifted his backpack stuffed with jars and bags for collecting samples, a notebook for writing his findings and for sketching, and his nets and traps. He shouldered his rifle and we were off, back across this frightful lava landscape.

The giant lizards and steaming lava that so frightened me delighted Charles Darwin. He must have stopped 30 times to stare at something and say, "Would you look at that! I've never seen anything like it anywhere else in the world."

Up a small rise at the upper edge of the twisted lava field, we reached a grove of taller trees filled with birds. It was hard to hear each other talk over the noise of a thousand chirping finches.

Mr. Darwin stared first at the birds on one branch and then he turned to study another like a kid staring at different tubs in an ice cream shop. "They're finches all right. But their beaks are larger and rounder than other finches we've seen."

Then he froze, staring hard at one small group of bright yellow finches near the end of a long, waving branch. "Look," he whispered. "Those are eating. Can you see what they're eating?"

"It looks like red berries, Mr. Darwin."

"My word, you're right, Jason. Imagine that! A finch eating berries. We need some sketches and samples."

He dropped to the hard ground and took out his notebook. He ripped out several sheets and handed them to me. "You draw. You're better than I am."

While I carefully drew the birds and their unique beaks, he wrote quick notes on what we saw. "Done, Jason? Good. Now for some samples." As Darwin raced, net in hand, to snare the needed samples, the great flock of frightened birds leapt into the air over our heads, darting back and forth like a brightly colored cloud.

Back on board the *Beagle*, Mr. Darwin took his two new finches straight to his crowded cabin, one deck below the Captain's room. Within an hour he discovered that these finches seemed to eat nothing but berries. "Think of it, Jason," he said. "Everywhere else on earth finches eat seeds—except in these crazy islands."

"But *some* of them eat seeds," I reminded him.

From *Stepping Stones to Science*. © 1997 Kendall Haven. Teacher Ideas Press. (800) 237-6124.

He nodded. "Yes. We found those seed-eaters on Chatham Island, wasn't it?" (Chatham Island was the first of the Galapagos Islands we visited.)

But then he pointed at the drawings, notes, and beak samples laid out across the floor. "Here on James Island, berries are plentiful and the finches have long, rounded beaks. Those that lived where insects were plentiful had slender, more pointed beaks—beaks just fit for catching insects. And those from the west side of Chatham Island, who seemed to live off nuts, all had thicker, heavier beaks. Again, just the perfect beak for cracking nuts."

He leaned back against the cabin bulk head and sighed, swaying slightly with the gentle rocking of the ship.

"The question, Jason, is how did all these different finches come to be here, when in all the rest of the world finches all have the same shape of beak and eat only seeds?"

We sat in silence through the muggy stillness of evening. The slight breeze seemed only to blow hotter air in upon us. I suggested, "Maybe they just grew here."

Mr. Darwin nodded. "Exactly, Jason! Each species seems to have evolved, or adapted, to an individual island and its unique food supply. Once a flock settled on a particular island, they seem to have begun to change—to adapt—to the unique conditions of that island. Oh, it may well have taken thousands of years for them to evolve this much."

I interrupted. "You mean these birds haven't always looked like they do now?"

"I'm sure not, Jason. I can see no other explanation," he said. "And with each passing generation those individuals with beaks best suited for their particular island survived best. So that over a long period of time more than a dozen separate species of finches have evolved. It would seem that the Earth's species continually change, adapt, and evolve to best suit themselves to their environment."

That night, with the tropical heat bearing down and the gently rocking *Beagle* beneath us, this idea seemed like a simple, obvious truth about the wondrous nature we looked upon every day with our own eyes. It didn't feel like a revolutionary idea. Who could have imagined the great uproar this simple idea would create once Mr. Darwin published it in his books, *The Voyage of the Beagle* and *Origin of Species*? But that is another story.

■ ■ ■

From *Stepping Stones to Science*. © 1997 Kendall Haven. Teacher Ideas Press. (800) 237-6124.

Follow-Up Activities

Charles Darwin struggled to understand how, over long periods of time, species of plant and animals had changed and adapted to their specific surroundings.

Here are some fun, easy, and powerful activities you can do to better understand the traits that mark you as part of your specific family, and what it takes to make one species different from another.

Topics to Talk About

1. **What Are Characteristics?** We say that species are different because they show distinct characteristics, or traits. What are these characteristics? (*Any physical common characteristic can mark one group as a separate species. Darwin used beak size and shape to differentiate a dozen species of finches unique to the Galapagos Islands. The unique beak shape of each group of birds was a characteristic Darwin used to differentiate one group, or species, from the others.*) Will *any* characteristic define a species? (*No. It has to be one that all members of the species uniquely hold in common and one that marks this species as different from all others. For example, each of Darwin's species of finches have wings and feathers. But neither characteristic is unique to any one species. Neither could be used to define a species.*) What characteristics do you possess? (*Your height, bone type, nose shape, eye color, hair color, lip shape, and 10,000 other traits are all characteristics you inherited from previous generations in your family.*)

2. **What Makes One Species Different from Another?** It's easy to tell the difference between an elephant and a goldfish. But what separates two species of owl or two species of beetle? (*There has to be at least one significant characteristic common to all members of a group, and which is uniquely different from other groups for that group to be called a different species.*) What about between people? Are the differences between people enough to call different groups separate species? (*No. The differences between different groups of people are too small to qualify as separate species.*)

3. **Do People Evolve?** How? How quickly? (*Yes. Humans, like most other species, are continually evolving as our environment and interactions with other species change. For example, over time humans are growing taller. People are significantly taller than they were even 100 years ago. In general, evolutionary changes happen very slowly, over thousands of years. They are hard to notice during only one lifetime.*) Are other species evolving around us? Can you see it happen? (*Virtually all species evolve. Some evolve very slowly. Many shark species have changed little over the past ten million years. Some, such as some viruses and crop pests, are evolving so rapidly that scientists can barely keep up with their changes. Some bacterial pests, for example, have evolved new ways to protect themselves against pesticides in less than one growing season.*)

From *Stepping Stones to Science.* © 1997 Kendall Haven. Teacher Ideas Press. (800) 237-6124.

Activities to Do

1. Necessary Equipment:

   - Copies of "Student Worksheet," page 115

2. A "Look" from Your Past.

   Darwin studied plants and birds. He divided them into separate species according to specific, easily visible traits. Beak size and shape are two such traits. Humans, however, are much more difficult to study. Their genetic structure is incredibly complex. Traits can lie dormant for generations before surfacing, seemingly at random. Still, let's see if you can detect the principles of this process at work in your own family.

   - Create a family tree listing you, your brothers and sisters, your parents and their brothers and sisters, your grandparents, and your great-grandparents. Use the enclosed worksheet for this form or make your own.

   - As a class, select two physical characteristics you want to track. Each of these traits should be physically visible and easy to describe. Good example sets are hair color and eye color, or hair texture and nose shape. But other traits such as height could also be used.

   - Identify each selected trait for every person on your family tree. Use pictures and the memory of other family members for those you are not able to see directly.

   - Search for patterns and the flow of traits through your family tree. Identify dominant traits that show up over and over again. Often your family will already know these, calling them "family traits." Did you find recessive traits that surfaced only once, or just a few times? Can you predict any traits that the next generation of your family will probably exhibit?

   - This is an exercise in pattern identification. You are trying to track the flow of traits through your family. Did you find any traits so dominant that they always show up? Are there others that show up in only one person in your whole family?

   - It is also a chance to think about what makes a species unique. Moving beyond the two traits you tracked in this experiment, can you find traits that are dominant across whole segments of our population? Can you find universal human traits? What is it that makes humans a separate species? What are our closest neighbor species? How do they differ from humans?

From *Stepping Stones to Science.* © 1997 Kendall Haven. Teacher Ideas Press. (800) 237-6124.

STUDENT WORKSHEET
for Activities to Do
following a story about **Charles Darwin**

1. A Look from Your Past

For each person in your family tree below, fill in a name and list the two
characteristics your class has chosen to track.

Our class chose these two characteristics: 1. _____

2. _____

1.   1.   1.   1.   1.   1.   1.   1.
2.   2.   2.   2.   2.   2.   2.   2.
___   ___   ___   ___   ___   ___   ___   ___

Your Eight Great-Grandparents

1.   1.   1.   1.
2.   2.   2.   2.
___   ___   ___   ___

1.   1.   1.   1.   1.   1.   1.   1.
2.   2.   2.   2.   2.   2.   2.   2.
___   ___   ___   ___   ___   ___   ___   ___

Their Brothers   Your Four Grandparents   Their Brothers
& Sisters   & Sisters

1.   1.   1.   1.   1.   1.   1.   1.
2.   2.   2.   2.   2.   2.   2.   2.
___   ___   ___   ___   ___   ___   ___   ___

His Brothers & Sisters   Your Father   Your Mother   Her Brothers & Sisters

1.   1.   1.   1.
2.   2.   2.   2.
___   ___   ___   ___

You   Your Brothers & Sisters

From *Stepping Stones to Science*. © 1997 Kendall Haven. Teacher Ideas Press. (800) 237-6124.

Additional Reading

Good references in the children's library for further reading on evolution and on Darwin's experiments include:

Allan, Mea. *Darwin and His Flowers.* New York: Taplinger Publishing, 1977.

Altman, Linda. *Mr. Darwin's Voyage.* Morristown, NJ: Dillon Press, 1995.

Bowlby, John. *Charles Darwin: A New Life.* New York: W. W. Norton, 1990.

Browne, E. J. *Charles Darwin: A Biography.* New York: Knopf, 1995.

Darwin, Charles. *The Beagle Record.* Cambridge, England: Cambridge University Press, 1979.

De Camp, L. Sprague, and Catherine Crook De Camp. *Darwin and His Great Discovery.* New York: Macmillan, 1972.

Desmond, Adrian. *Darwin.* New York: Warner Books, 1992.

Evans, J. Edward. *Charles Darwin: Revolutionary Biologist.* Minneapolis, MN: Lerner, 1993.

Gallant, Roy. *Charles Darwin.* Garden City, NY: Doubleday, 1982.

Jastrow, Robert. *The Essential Darwin.* Boston: Little, Brown, 1984.

Johnson, Philip. *Darwin on Trial.* Washington, DC: Regency Gateway, 1991.

Mayr, Ernst. *One Long Argument: Charles Darwin and the Genesis of Modern Evolutionary Thought.* Cambridge, MA: Harvard University Press, 1991.

Milner, Richard. *Charles Darwin: Evolution of a Naturalist.* New York: Facts on File, 1993.

Parker, Steve. *Charles Darwin and Evolution.* New York: HarperCollins, 1992.

Quackenbush, Robert. *The Beagle and Mr. Flycatcher.* Englewood Cliffs, NJ: Prentice-Hall, 1983.

Sproule, Anna. *Charles Darwin: el cientifico que revoluciona los ideas tradicionales sobre el origen del hombre.* Madrid: Ediciones SM, 1990.

Steadman, David. *Galapagos: Discovery on Darwin's Islands.* Washington, DC: Smithsonian Institution Press, 1988.

Stebbins, G. Ledyard. *Darwin to DNA, Molecules to Humanity.* San Francisco: W. H. Freeman, 1982.

White, Michael. *Darwin: A Life in Science.* New York: Dutton, 1996.

Consult your librarian for additional titles.

"Green Pea, Yellow Pea"

A Story of Gregor Mendel's Discovery of Heredity in 1865

➤ A Point to Ponder

A pre-story question to focus student attention and interest on the story's central science theme—After all the centuries that people have been living and reproducing and mixing on this planet, why don't all people look alike? Why don't you look just like your parents?

➤ Science Curriculum Links

This story deals with the life science concepts of heredity and of dominant and recessive traits. Why do we have some features like one parent, some like the other, and some like a grandparent, great-grandparent, or no one in the family at all? How do those traits come to us? What makes them show up in some generations and not in others?

Use this story to introduce the concept of heredity (and how all living organisms use genes to pass traits to the next generation), to expand a unit on plants and how they grow, or as an excellent example of the scientific process of experiment and observation at work.

➤ Key Picture-Maker Words

The following words create mental pictures important to the understanding of this story. However, not all your students may be familiar with each of them. Here are ways to quickly review these words and concepts to ensure that your students get the most out of these moments in science.

1. **Monastery:** A monastery is a place for religious monks (men) to live and work apart from the rest of the world. A similar place for nuns (women) is called a convent.

2. **Abbot and Bishop:** These are the titles of two senior positions in the Catholic church structure. In this story an Abbot runs the Bruun Monastery. He is the equivalent of a store manager. The Bishop is in charge of

all the church activities and facilities within a large region. He is the equivalent of a company president.

At your school, who would be the equivalent of an Abbot? (the Principal) Who would be the equivalent of a Bishop? (the Superintendent of Schools)

3. **Trait:** A trait is an identifying characteristic. The shape of your nose is a trait. Many members of a family often have the same shape nose. That is, they show the same nose trait. The color of your hair and eyes are traits, as are your height and the size of your bones. Besides these visible traits you inherit from your ancestors, you also inherit many invisible traits. In all, you inherit thousands of traits from your parents, your grand-parents, and the many generations that have come before.

Have your students list the most common physical traits in their families.

Do only people inherit traits? What about birds? What about weeds? All plants and animals inherit traits from past generations.

4. **Heredity:** The sum of all the traits passed to you from previous genera-tions is your heredity. Heredity is the passing on of specific traits from generation to generation. Gregor Mendel studied heredity. That means he studied how traits were passed from one generation to the next, and on to the next.

5. **Crossed (Cross-breed):** The set of traits you carry is a mix of the traits that came to you from your father, and the traits which came to you from your mother. This is also true for plants.

To cross-breed means to use one plant with one kind of trait as the father plant for a new generation of plants, and to use a plant with a different kind of trait for the mother plant. The new plants then possess both kinds of traits.

Gregor Mendel carefully cross-bred his pea plants. He used a tall kind of pea plant (a plant with the trait of being tall) as the father plant, and a short pea plant (a plant with the trait of being short) for the mother plant.

The next generation of pea plants thus carried both the trait for being tall and the trait for being short. Gregor Mendel wanted to see which trait would control the growth of the new plants, or if they would be controlled by a combination of the two traits.

6. **Generation:** Within a family it is easy to identify all the members of one generation. Counting from your great-grandmother, for example, your grandparents and their brothers and sisters are the first generation; your parents, their brothers, sisters, and cousins, are the second generation; and you, your brothers, sisters, and cousins are the third generation.

A generation is that group of beings who represent a single step in the line of descendants from a single ancestor. It's harder to identify a generation of Americans, because at any given moment there are Americans of every possible age.

It is easier to identify the generations of a plant. The annual cycle of warm, summer growing season and cold, winter dormant season makes every plant species start a new generation at the beginning of the spring/summer growing season. Because they all start a new generation at the same time, it's easier to track each generation.

7. **Dominant:** *Dominant* means to dominate, to control, or to exert the controlling influence over an organism or group and determine its growth or outcome.

   Your teacher is dominant in the classroom. That lets her lead and direct you in your learning. Some animals are dominant in their environment. Black and brown bears are dominant in the mountainous environments of the western United States. Lions are said to be kings, or dominant, in the African grasslands.

   In any group, does one individual rise to be the dominant leader, the "king of the hill?" Does it happen with your friends?

   Inside everybody, traits also struggle to be dominant. You may carry four or five traits for the shape of your nose. But only one will be dominant and determine your nose's final shape.

8. **Recessive:** The opposite of dominant is *recessive*. While each dominant trait determines what your body will look like, the recessive traits you carry don't determine anything. Recessive traits are the traits that lost out to the bully trait and have to sit on the sidelines and do nothing but wait to be passed on to a new generation where they will try to be dominant all over again.

"Green Pea, Yellow Pea"

Early one morning in May 1865, the Bishop of Prague's open-topped carriage rolled up the sloping dirt road, up to the main gate to the Austrian Monastery of Bruun. The Abbot and his monks eagerly assembled to meet this important church official.

By mid-afternoon the Bishop's tour of the monastery led him to the gardens and fields, including the small plot used by one of the monks, Father Gregor Mendel, for his scientific experiments on heredity. He studied how specific traits are passed from one individual to the next generation, and through future generations into a whole population.

Strolling beside the neat rows of pea plants in the warm sun, the Bishop smiled. "Ah, peas for dinner, I see."

"Oh, no, your grace!" exclaimed plump Father Mendel, nervously wiping his small round glasses. "No one eats these peas."

"In heaven's name, why not?" demanded the Bishop.

"They're my experiment," answered Father Mendel.

The bishop glared at Father Mendel and his rows of peas. "What experiment could possibly be more important than my dinner?"

The Abbot wrung his hands, fearing the anger of the Bishop would be turned against the whole monastery. But Father Mendel was not afraid. "These peas are my experiment in heredity."

"Heredity, you say?" snapped the bishop. "I thought that English fellow—Darwin—settled everything about heredity."

As the Bishop rocked back and forth, hands clasped behind his back, his face upturned to soak in the spring sunshine, Father Mendel explained that Darwin's work on evolution had, indeed, explained that individual traits *were* passed from one generation to the next, and that these traits could *evolve*, or change, over time. But Darwin never discovered *how* characteristics are passed down through the generations, some to dominate in every generation, some to randomly pop up now and then. Why and how did this happen? That was what Father Mendel wanted to study.

"Yes, I see," said the Bishop with a slight yawn. "And how does it happen?"

Father Mendel shrugged his shoulders and turned his eyes to the rows of pea plants just beginning to stretch their vine-like arms up and around the supporting trellises. "The answer, your grace, is somewhere in my new crop of peas."

From *Stepping Stones to Science.* © 1997 Kendall Haven. Teacher Ideas Press. (800) 237-6124.

Continuing on his official tour, the Bishop grunted over his shoulder. "Peas. Such an odd place to look for heredity. They'd do much better as my dinner."

On a hazy August day that same year, church business brought the Bishop back to Bruun. Near the end of his stay at the monastery he found Gregor Mendel weeding in his garden plot. "Ah, Father Mendel," he smiled. "Have your peas whispered any secrets to you this summer?"

The Abbot hissed at Mendel, "Be nice to the Bishop, and don't make him mad this time!"

Mendel eagerly rubbed his hands together. "I will show you, your grace."

Pointing at a row of tall, straight pea plants, Mendel said, "I cross-bred a row of—"

"You did what?" interrupted the bishop.

Mendel explained. "Each plant needs two parents, your grace, just like humans do. Cross-breeding means that one of the parents had one trait, such as being tall, while the other parent showed a different trait, such as being short. Thus, each new plant received both the trait for being tall and the trait for being short. That's cross-breeding."

"I see," said the bishop. "You should have said so in the first place."

"I did," muttered Father Mendel.

"Be nice!" hissed the Abbot.

Father Mendel continued. "So, your grace, I cross-bred tall pea plants with short pea plants. What kind of pea plants do you think grew from those seeds?"

The Bishop sounded thoroughly bored. "A row of medium-size plants, I suppose. Science is so dull, Father Mendel."

"Wrong!" corrected Mendel. "I got *all* tall plants. And when I planted the seeds from those tall plants what do you think I got in the third generation?"

The Bishop waved his hand in a careless way. "More tall plants, I suppose." Then he added, "This really isn't very interesting work, Father Mendel. You should go back to growing peas for dinner."

"Wrong again!" shouted Father Mendel triumphantly.

"Don't shout at the Bishop!" hissed the Abbot.

Father Mendel explained, "I got *mostly* tall plants in the third generation with a few short plants. The short trait returned in the third generation."

"Really?" asked the Bishop, interested in spite of himself. "But you got no medium-height plants?"

Father Mendel was already pointing at the next row and the next experiment. "And now guess what happened when I cross-bred yellow peas with green peas?"

"Yellow-green peas, I suppose," answered the Bishop.

"Wrong!" shouted Father Mendel.

"Stop shouting!" yelled the Abbot.

Father Mendel continued. "I got *all* yellow peas in the second generation. But when I planted the seeds from those yellow peas, in the third generation I got *mostly* yellow with a few green peas. But never a yellow-green. The traits don't mix."

"Really? Never?" The Bishop was fascinated. "And which one tastes better? That is the point, I assume: to produce a tastier pea?"

But Mendel was lost back into other pages of his journal. "Here it is again! I cross-bred smooth-skinned with wrinkled-skinned peas. In the second generation I got all smooth-skinned peas. In the third generation I got *mostly* smooth-skinned peas. But again I got a few wrinkled-skin peas. The wrinkled-skin trait had returned."

"Really? The same pattern every time?" asked the Bishop, finally finding something in Mendel's work more important than dinner. "Remarkable. That would seem to defy the very laws of nature."

The wheels were spinning inside Gregor's head that night as he paced across his small room. Over and over he muttered his findings to himself, hoping they'd finally make sense. "I cross-bred tall plants with short plants. The second generation had both the trait for being tall and the trait for being short."

Hands clasped behind him, Gregor continued to pace and mutter. "But none of them grew short. They *all* grew tall. But in all future generations the short plant trait returned and there were a few short plants and mostly tall ones."

He stopped and sighed. Then continued his steady pacing. "Is the Bishop right? Does it *defy* nature that it always comes out the same?"

Around midnight, in a sudden flash of understanding, the answer came to him. He had spent six years growing, watering, weeding, and carefully breeding pea plants in his garden plot. In his mind, all that work simplified to one simple mathematical principle.

"How odd," he thought. "It took six years to discover the obvious. It doesn't defy nature. It defines nature's way!"

For each characteristic, he knew, every plant inherited one trait (or gene) from the father plant and one from the mother plant. But what if, for each pair of these traits, one trait were always stronger, more powerful (dominant), and one always weaker (recessive)? When both traits were present, the stronger (dominant) trait, like a neighborhood bully, would push the weaker (recessive) trait aside, and the plant would grow following only the dominant trait. But the weaker trait would still be there, not appearing in the plant, but hiding. It would still be there to pass on to future generations.

Peas, mathematics, and a seventh year of experiments in the garden confirmed Father Mendel's answer. Traits do not mix. They are passed from generation to generation and appear only when they are dominant, or stronger, in an individual plant. All other traits remain hidden, unused, waiting to be passed on again. Traits from countless ancestors flow into each of us, in separate packages called "genes," unblended for us to pass on even if the traits don't "show" in our generation.

In the fall of 1866 Father Mendel excitedly presented his findings to the Bruun Society for Natural Studies. "Inherited traits follow simple mathematical laws, either dominating or recessing in any given generation," he told them, expecting the light of understanding to glow with excitement in their eyes.

He got only blank stares. "Father Mendel. Mathematics and peas have absolutely nothing to do with each other. What, in heaven's name, are you talking about?"

No amount of explaining and demonstrating made Mendel's generation understand. But 34 years later, in 1900, the Dutch scientist Hugo de Vries realized Mendel's great gift to the world with his insights on heredity. But that is another story.

■ ■ ■

Follow-Up Activities

Gregor Mendel struggled to understand how traits are passed down from one generation to the next, from parent to child.

Here are some fun, easy, and powerful activities you can do to better understand the concept of heredity, and of how dominant and recessive traits are passed from one generation to the next.

Topics to Talk About

1. What is heredity? (*Heredity is all the characteristics and tendencies we inherit from our ancestors.*) What does it do for us? (*Most of who you are, what you are like, what you like, and your physical abilities and traits are determined by what was passed to you from previous generations of your family. All these characteristics are what we call heredity. Heredity determines your tendency to be sick, your sports ability, much of your school ability, and many of your likes and dislikes, as well as your physical appearance.*) What do we get through heredity? (*We receive many signals from past generations for every physical characteristic—from eye color to height to hair texture—to every tendency, every facet of your personality, and every facet of your growth and life.*)

2. Why is heredity so hard to study? Why don't we already know exactly how traits are passed from generation to generation? (*There are many good reasons. First, the genes that carry our heredity information are incredibly complex. There are millions of genes, each controlling different aspects of our lives. Moreover, not all the genes you carry are active. Many lie dormant for all your life and do nothing. Yet they look exactly like the active genes. Second, genes are microscopic. They are almost impossible to actually see. Third, there are no markings on a gene. They do not carry neat labels for scientists to read. They are long chains of molecules. It took many years of research to even begin to understand how they work.*)

3. Why do most heredity studies look at plants or flies instead of at people? (*Here are five reasons. We can't experiment on people; we can on plants. Plants have far fewer genes to track and separate. Plants are faster to study, as they live through a generation in a year or less, while human generations occur every 20 to 25 years. Plants can be isolated and carefully followed. Humans cannot. Finally, plants can be torn apart, ground up, and analyzed. Humans cannot.*)

Activities to Do

1. Necessary Equipment:
   - 22 small paper bags (the "lunch bag" size works best)
   - 32 yellow and 32 blue marbles, all the same size
   - Copies of "Student Worksheet," page 127

2. The Dominant Probability.

   Gregor Mendel found simple patterns in the way traits are passed from one generation to the next. He discovered that one trait for each characteristic was given to a new plant by each parent. If those two traits differed, one tended to be dominant (direct the development of that new plant), and one recessive (not appear or not actively present in the new plant, but still carried by that plant).

   With that information he found he could predict what traits future-generation plants would show. Let's try an experiment to see if you can also determine how heredity works.

   - Label two paper bags "First Generation Father" and "First Generation Mother." Place eight yellow marbles in the "Father" bag and eight blue marbles in the "Mother" bag. Each marble represents a possible trait for the plant's color characteristic. For this experiment, assume that the blue marble trait is dominant and the yellow marble trait is recessive. That is, if any plant has any of the blue marble trait, it will be a blue plant. Plants will only be yellow if they receive nothing but yellow marble trait.

   - Finally, label four bags as Second Generation Plants #1, #2, #3, and #4. This setup is shown on the enclosed worksheet. You can use this sheet to record your results for this experiment.

   - The first thing to do is to pollinate the second-generation plants with traits from father and mother plants. To do this, have one student close his or her eyes, reach into the First Generation Mother bag, draw out a marble (trait), and drop it into the first of the Second Generation Plant bags. In the same way, draw marbles for the other three Second Generation bags.

   - A second student should do the same thing for the traits each second-generation plant receives from the Father bag.

   - Now look in each of the second generation plants to see which traits they have received. One blue and one yellow, right? Therefore, all four second generation plants will be blue plants—that is, show the dominant, blue trait. This is what Mendel predicted.

3. Third Time's the Charm.

   - Now let's see what happens with the *third* generation. Label 16 bags as Third Generation Plant #1 through #16. Remember, each Second Generation plant has an equal number of yellow and blue traits, and each will pass on only one trait to each of its third generation offspring. So each has an equal chance of passing on either a yellow or blue trait to any of the Third Generation plants.

   - Load eight yellow and eight blue marbles into each of the four Second Generation bags as an initial stock of traits, or genes, to pass on. This is enough marbles to ensure that each time a marble is drawn from a Second Generation bag it will have approximately the same chance of being either yellow or blue.

- Now pollinate the Third Generation. Remember, each Third Generation plant (bag) must receive one trait (marble) from each of two different Second Generation plants. You also must make sure each Second Generation plant pollinates the same number of Third Generation plants. Finally, you want to ensure that each possible combination of Second Generation parents is used—as closely as possible—the same number of times.

- Take as much time as you need to figure out how to pollinate the Third Generation following these three rules. Note that some Third Generation plants will have the same two Second Generation parents.

- Write the numbers of the two Second Generation parents (bags) on each Third Generation bag. An example of a numbering scheme that works is: 1-2, 1-3, 1-4, 1-2, 2-1, 2-3, 2-4, 2-3, 3-1, 3-2, 3-4, 3-4, 4-1, 4-2, 4-3, 4-1.

- Have students, with eyes closed, pick marbles (traits) one at a time from each Second Generation parent and drop them into the appropriate Third Generation bags.

- Assign one student as "Mother Nature" to oversee this process and ensure that one marble from each of the correct Second Generation bags is deposited in each of the correct Third Generation bags.

- Which traits did each third generation plant (bag) receive? Each Third Generation bag should have two marbles (traits), one from each of two different Second Generation parents. Take the two marbles from each Third Generation bag and decide if that plant will be a yellow or blue plant. Write the color of each plant on its bag. How many Third Generation plants of each color did you have? Gregor Mendel decided that, on average, you should have twelve blue and four yellow plants. On the worksheet, record the traits received by each Third Generation plant (bag) and the color that plant will become.

- Did your Third Generation differ from Mendel's three-to-one ratio? Watch for patterns to emerge in your bags as they did for Mendel in his rows of pea plants. Those same patterns operate to direct human heredity, or the passing on of traits through human families. Those patterns are very difficult to detect in humans, however, because there is such a complex variety of possible traits that could be carried by, and passed on by, parents, grandparents, and great-grandparents.

- Can you find examples in your own family, or in the flowers and plants around you, of dominant traits that show up in plant after plant and family member after family member? Can you find recessive traits that have appeared in one person or plant that didn't appear in either parent?

STUDENT WORKSHEET
for Activities to Do
following a story about **Gregor Mendel**

1. Playing Mother Nature.

FIRST GENERATION

First Generation Father (Blue)

First Generation Mother (Yellow)

SECOND GENERATION

2nd Gen. Plant #1
1.
2.
Color:

2nd Gen. Plant #2
1.
2.
Color:

2nd Gen. Plant #3
1.
2.
Color:

2nd Gen. Plant #4
1.
2.
Color:

THIRD GENERATION

3rd Gen # 1
Parents: __&__
1.
2
Color: ____

3rd Gen # 2
Parents: __&__
1.
2
Color: ____

3rd Gen # 3
Parents: __&__
1.
2
Color: ____

3rd Gen # 4
Parents: __&__
1.
2
Color: ____

3rd Gen # 5
Parents: __&__
1.
2
Color: ____

3rd Gen # 6
Parents: __&__
1.
2
Color: ____

3rd Gen # 7
Parents: __&__
1.
2
Color: ____

3rd Gen # 8
Parents: __&__
1.
2
Color: ____

3rd Gen # 9
Parents: __&__
1.
2
Color: ____

3rd Gen # 10
Parents: __&__
1.
2
Color: ____

3rd Gen # 11
Parents: __&__
1.
2
Color: ____

3rd Gen # 12
Parents: __&__
1.
2
Color: ____

3rd Gen # 13
Parents: __&__
1.
2
Color: ____

3rd Gen # 14
Parents: __&__
1.
2
Color: ____

3rd Gen # 15
Parents: __&__
1.
2
Color: ____

3rd Gen # 16
Parents: __&__
1.
2
Color: ____

Additional Reading

Good references in the children's library for further reading on heredity, on human traits, and on Mendel's experiments include:

Asimov, Isaac. *How Did We Find Out About Genes?* New York: Walker, 1978.

Bendick, Jeanne. *How Heredity Works.* New York: Parents' Magazine Press, 1975.

Bornstein, Sandy. *What Makes You What You Are.* Englewood Cliffs, NJ: Julian Messner, 1989.

Byczynski, Lynn. *Genetics, Nature's Blueprints.* San Diego, CA: Lucent Books, 1991.

Dawkins, Richard. *The Selfish Gene.* New York: Oxford University Press, 1989.

Edelson, Edward. *Genetics and Heredity.* New York: Chelsea House, 1990.

Edlin, Gordon. *Genetic Principles.* Boston: Jones and Bartlett, 1984.

Fradin, Dennis. *Heredity.* Chicago: Childrens Press, 1987.

Gardner, Eldon. *Principles of Genetics.* New York: John Wiley, 1984.

George, Wilma. *Gregor Mendel and Heredity.* Howe, England: Wayland, 1975.

Morrison, Velma. *There's Only One You.* New York: Messner, 1978.

Olby, Robert. *Origins of Mendelism.* New York: Schocken Books, 1966.

Oleksy, Walter. *Miracle of Genetics.* Chicago: Childrens Press, 1986.

Patent, Dorothy. *Grandfather's Nose: Why We Look Alike or Different.* New York: F. Watts, 1989.

Pomerantz, Charlotte. *Why You Look Like You, Whereas I Tend to Look Like Me.* New York: W. R. Scott, 1969.

Sootin, Harry. *Gregor Mendel: Father of the Science of Genetics.* New York: Vanguard Press, 1959.

Webb, Robert. *Gregor Mendel and Heredity.* New York: F. Watts, 1973.

Webster, Gary. *The Man Who Found Out Why.* New York: Hawthorne Press, 1963.

Consult your librarian for additional titles.

Shark "Bait"

A Story of Eugenie Clark's Discovery of Shark Intelligence in 1956

➤ A Point to Ponder

A pre-story question to focus student attention and interest on the story's central science theme—Do you think sharks are smart? As smart as a dog? As smart as a seagull? As smart as a cat? Are all animals smart? How do you know?

➤ Science Curriculum Links

This story deals with the life science concepts of animal intelligence, patterns of animal behavior, and how humans interact with other living things. How smart are animals? How can humans measure that intelligence?

Use this story as part of a unit on the oceans, on general biology, on intelligence, or on famous American scientists.

➤ Key Picture-Maker Words

The following words create mental pictures important to the understanding of this story. However, not all your students may be familiar with each of them. Here are ways to quickly review these words and concepts to ensure that your students get the most out of these moments in science.

1. **Marker Buoy:** A buoy is a floating frame anchored to sit in one spot in the water. Marker buoys are placed along channels and in open water so that a boat can get back to the same spot time after time.

    Commonly, marker buoys are metal tube frames, most often painted red, standing six to ten feet high and three to six feet across at the water line, with blinking lights on top and bells or horns so ships can hear them in the dark or fog.

    You can see marker buoys around harbors or marinas, in many lakes and rivers, and in the open ocean near harbor or bay entrances.

2. **Senseless:** Literally, senseless means to not have any sense. Commonly it means foolish or stupid.

    In this story, one character says that sharks are senseless killers. What he really means is that he believes they act purely on instinct: swimming, hunting, and attacking without thinking or planning.

3. **Shark Pen:** A large, cement, usually outdoor pool filled with salt water where sharks are kept for study. Similar to, but much bigger than, a private swimming pool, they usually have no shallow end and are ringed by a waist-high wall to keep people from slipping and falling in with the sharks.

4. **Intelligence:** Can you learn something new? Can you learn it easily? Are some people better or faster at learning something new, or at figuring out what to do in a new situation?

    The ability to do those things is called *intelligence*. What common words can you think of that mean almost the same thing? *Wise*, *smart*, and *brainy* are three words that have meanings close to *intelligent*. Can you think of others?

5. **Journal:** As used in this story, a journal is a blank book where private notes and thoughts are kept. A journal is like a diary. Many people write their thoughts each day into a diary. Many scientists keep a journal for each experiment or research project and write their findings, observations, and thoughts in the journal each day.

    Any blank-paged notebook can be a journal. You can find hardbound journals in stationary stores. Bring your own journal in to show your students, if you have one.

6. **Target Board:** A target is something you aim at. A target board is a wooden target.

    In this story, Eugenie Clark makes a wooden target board for her sharks to aim at and bump into to let her know that they are hungry and want to be fed. Bumping the target board was the signal for Eugenie to give them food. Seeing if the sharks were smart enough to figure that out was part of her test to see how intelligent sharks are.

7. **Hovered:** Hummingbirds hover in front of a flower. Helicopters hover over the ground when they sit, motionless, in the air.

    To hover means to flutter, suspended in air or water, remaining in one place. What else can hover? What have you seen hovering?

    As used in this story, *hover* also means to hang in a state of uncertainty, to be unsure of what to do.

    Near the end of this story, one of the sharks "hovers." See if both meanings for *hover* fit with what you think is happening to this shark.

Shark "Bait"

Beryl Chadwick shut down the rumbling engine of the research boat. The boat nudged against a red marker buoy, anchored in the open sea. He listened to the gentle slap of ocean waves against the boat and to the cry of circling seagulls.

"We're at the first buoy, Dr. Clark," he announced. It was April 1956. The weather looked good as far as he could see across the blue waters of the Florida Strait.

Beryl Chadwick had been hired to help Dr. Eugenie Clark collect fish species native to Florida and the Caribbean area. This was his first collection trip, and he didn't want any problems with storms.

He saw Dr. Clark walk onto the boat's rear deck wearing a scuba diving suit. "Oh, no, no, no, no, Dr. Clark," he pleaded. "Don't dive here. There are sharks here!"

Dr. Clark laughed and tucked her brown hair under her diving hood. "That's why we're here."

"But . . . but Dr. Clark!" Beryl protested. "You could *meet* a shark down there." He pointed with his thumb over the side of the lab's boat.

Eugenie (Genie to everyone who knew her) just nodded. "I better. That's what I came for."

Beryl had been a fishing boat captain for 30 years. He knew the waters. He knew the fish. And he knew the sharks. "But sharks are mindless *killers*. How will you protect yourself?"

Genie's face spread into a wide, friendly smile, and she held up a pressurized can, like an aerosol spray can. "I'll spray some MS-222 down its throat. It knocks a shark unconscious and makes it much easier to bring in."

Beryl's face wrinkled up with fear. "You're going to reach out right next to its teeth and spray stuff down its throat? Oh, no, no, no, no! This is a bad idea."

Genie adjusted her face mask and dropped into the warm blue waters off the Florida Keys, still smiling.

"A bad, bad, *very* bad idea!" Beryl called after her.

As the sun set that evening, Genie and Beryl stood on the cement walkway surrounding the Cape Hays Marine Lab shark pen. The female shark Genie had caught that afternoon (a kind called a "lemon" shark)

---

seemed to stagger as it slowly swam back and forth, still groggy from Genie's well-aimed spray of MS-222.

"She'll be fine," Genie nodded with satisfaction. "I think I'll name her Rosie." Rosie was the fourth shark in the pen.

Beryl Chadwick gruffly crossed his arms, still angry that she dove after he warned her not to. "Sharks are vicious, senseless killers," he repeated.

Genie paused, thinking. "I wonder if they really are senseless."

"Oh, yes, yes, yes," he reassured her.

"I wonder . . ." repeated Genie, realizing no one had ever bothered to find out. "I wonder. . . ."

Every shark study Genie had seen described shark behavior, how sharks act. No one had ever thought to see if sharks were smart. No one had ever tried to find out if sharks could think and learn.

"Beryl," she said. "Let's find out just how smart sharks are."

Beryl Chadwick groaned. "Oh, no, no, no, Dr. Clark. Another bad, bad idea. Who wants to know if sharks are smart?"

"I do," smiled Genie.

But how could she find out how smart a shark was? She couldn't ask sharks to take a test or answer questions. She couldn't send them to obedience school like a dog. What *could* she do to test a shark's intelligence?

Genie found a square wooden board and painted it bright white. Then she attached a piece of fish to it.

"What's that?" asked Beryl.

"It's called a target board," answered Genie.

Beryl scowled suspiciously. "A target for what?"

Genie laughed. "When one of the sharks comes for the food, it has to bump this target with its nose in order to lock its teeth on the food and pull it free. That bump will set off a bell. Once one shark takes some food, I'll quickly reload the wooden target with a fresh piece for another shark."

Beryl continued to scowl. "Still sounds like a bad, bad idea."

Time and time again, as the four lemon sharks drifted in lazy circles, one would curve off and rush at the target board and its tasty fish reward. Clang! went the bell.

First the female named Rosie, then Hazel, then one of the two males drove at Genie's white board. Clang! Clang! Day after day she fed the sharks by hooking hunks of fish on the target board. Clang! Clang!

"Too much clanging," complained Beryl. "It gives me a headache."

Genie laughed. "It's worth a headache if it teaches the sharks to think of the bell when they think of food."

Beryl shook his head. "I don't care what a shark thinks—as long as it doesn't think about eating me."

"Remember," said Genie. "We want to see if the sharks can learn a pattern. They bump the target board. They hear the bell. Then they get food. Let's see if they've learned to use that pattern. Tomorrow I'll move the fish reward and see if they can still remember to bump the target board and ring the bell."

The next day, instead of hooking fish hunks directly to the target board, Genie hid the tasty fish reward behind a sturdy iron fence. Then she slid the fence and fish a few feet to one side of her target board. The sharks couldn't reach the tempting fish unless Genie lifted the iron fence that hid it. Only when a shark remembered to use the established pattern (nose the target and clang the bell), would Genie lift the iron fence and let that shark get some fish.

At first the sharks hungrily attacked straight at the iron fence, bashing long dents into it, twisting and bending individual bars, gnawing at the metal, breaking their razor-teeth, trying to get at the fish behind.

Then Hazel seemed to give up and glide slowly out to the middle of their pen, her tail rhythmically swishing back and forth. She hesitated, as if thinking. Up on the walkway Genie held her breath. Would Hazel remember the pattern and ring the bell?

Yes! She drove straight at the old, wooden target. Clang! Genie lifted a section of the iron fence and Hazel swam off with a large hunk of tuna.

An amazed Beryl Chadwick slowly shook his head. "Maybe they're not so dumb after all."

Rosie was the second shark to figure out how to get some fish. She swam hard at the target board. Clang! Genie actually cheered. While Rosie ate, Genie entered careful notes in her experiment journal.

For six days Genie slowly inched the iron fence and the fish reward hidden behind it around the tank, farther and farther from the white target board and bell. None of the four sharks cared. Clang! They had learned exactly what to do. Each shark nosed into the target every time before turning to rush for their fish reward.

Within two weeks the sharks had learned to bump the target board, ring the bell, and then swim all the way across their pen and wait for a treat to be thrown to them by one of the staff biologists.

"It's amazing," said the lab director.

"Remarkable work," said marine biologists all over the world.

"I think it's a bad, bad, very bad idea to teach a shark to eat," grumbled Beryl Chadwick.

Genie still worried about her experiment. Did her sharks *really* understand that they used a pattern of different, individual steps in order to be fed? How could she be sure?

"Who cares?" asked Beryl. "You've got sharks doing circus tricks."

Genie answered, "Remember, we're here to find out how smart sharks are. I need to know if they are smart enough to really understand the pattern they use to get fed."

Three days later Rosie gave Genie her answer. Paul, one of the males, drove hard at the target board to call for a snack. He slammed into the target board. The bell clanged wildly. Paul hit the board so hard, he knocked the bell loose.

No one noticed until Rosie nosed the target for a treat of her own. No bell. Rosie turned to streak across the pen for her reward. Then she stopped. Something was wrong. She hadn't heard the familiar bell. She spun around and nosed the target again. Still no bell.

Rosie hovered in front of the target board a few seconds before ramming it again with her nose. Genie rushed over and clanged the bell herself. Satisfied, Rosie swam off for her reward.

Eugenie Clark cheered. The sharks *did* understand. They *were* smart, every bit as smart as many intelligent land animals. Rosie insisted on ringing the bell before she ate. That proved it.

Beryl slowly shook his head. "Maybe they are smart. But it's still a bad, bad, very bad idea to swim with one."

Eugenie Clark laughed and entered detailed notes in her experiment journal. Those notes changed the way the whole world looked at sharks, and led marine biologists to rethink their approach to research on many other oceanic species. But that's another story.

■ ■ ■

Follow-Up Activities

Dr. Eugenie Clark struggled to understand both how to measure an animal's intelligence and the intelligence, or learning capacity, of a common lemon shark.

Here are some fun, easy, and powerful activities you can do to better understand the difficulties of determining animal intelligence and how intelligent most animals really are.

Topics to Talk About

1. **What Is Intelligence:** How do we decide what makes something or someone smart? (*People can be given standard tests. Their results may be compared with the results by other people. We say that someone is smart if they do better on these tests than most people. Similarly, standard tests and "tricks" have been created to measure animal intelligence. Comparing how well one animal does on such a test with other members of its species, or with those in other species, gives us an idea of how smart that one animal is.*) What factors would you use?

2. **Measuring Intelligence:** How can we measure and compare the intelligence of our household pets? (*Measures you might use include the ability to learn and perform tricks, the ability to survive on their own in the wild, the ability to understand human commands, the ability to communicate their desires to humans, how sharp their various senses are, or the ability to understand and use objects from a human world.*) Which pets are most intelligent? Which are least intelligent? How do we know? How would you account for individual variation within a general group intelligence measure?

Activities to Do

1. Necessary Equipment:

   - Only paper and pencil are needed for this experiment. Other necessary equipment will be determined by the class during the experiment.

   - Copies of "Student Worksheet," page 137

2. What Is Intelligence?

   - In small groups (three to four students per group), make a list of what you think are the five smartest animals. Use the enclosed worksheet to write down your list. Next to each animal say why you think that animal is so intelligent. Compare lists between groups and see if you all used the same reasons (factors) for deciding which animals are intelligent.

- Write down the one factor you think is the most important in determining animal intelligence. Then vote as a class on the one factor from these lists that the class thinks is the single most important factor. How could you measure the factor you have chosen? Is there a test you could give to see which animals perform best at this intelligence factor?

- Eugenie Clark decided that the ability to learn and repeat a complex (three-step) series of related actions was the best test for her to use. She designed a test where her sharks had to push a piece of wood, listen for a bell to ring, and then swim somewhere else to receive a reward of fish.

3. Measuring Intelligence:

- Make a list of all household pets owned by members of your class. Your goal is to use the intelligence factor you selected in step #2 to see which of these species of pets will be crowned the most intelligent pet of the class.

- First, you must design a test to measure this factor. The test must be simple enough for you all to do it with your own pets. But it must be hard enough to really test the intelligence of your pets. Reread the story of Eugenie Clark and see how she created an intelligence test for her sharks.

- Write down your own idea for a pet intelligence test. Then compare everyone's idea in your class. As a class, agree on a test you will each use to test your pets.

- You must also decide how to tell when a pet is successful at this test. Is it speed, accuracy, or how often they do the test correctly?

- Test all class pets and write your results on the worksheet. It will be easiest for each student to actually perform the test at home with the help of parents. However, you could do it as a class project on a special science day at school.

- After completing the test, review the results for each pet. What makes doing the test hard? Did your pets cooperate? Did they try to do the test? Do you think they knew they were being tested? What does that tell you about their intelligence? Did all the members of any one pet species do equally well on your test? Is it hard to tell which pets did best on this test? Which pet won the title of most intelligent class pet?

- Look at your class's results. Could you have come to the same conclusion without a test? Could you have figured out which was most intelligent just by observing their natural behavior? Observe ants, flies, and snails. Which do you think are most intelligent? Why?

# STUDENT WORKSHEET
for Activities to Do
following a story about **Eugenie Clark**

1. I think the five smartest animals are:

	Animal	Reason
1.		
2.		
3.		
4.		
5.		

2. I think the one most important intelligence factor is: _____

_____

    The class picked this factor to use: _____

_____

3. My test to test pet intelligence is: _____

_____

    The class picked this test to use: _____

_____

4. Results with my pet: _____

_____

_____

_____

_____

Additional Reading

Good references in the children's library for further reading on animal intelligence and on Eugenie Clark's experiments include:

Arnold, Caroline. *Watch Out for Sharks!* New York: Clarion Books, 1991.

Behrens, June. *Sharks!* Chicago: Childrens Press, 1990.

Berger, Gilda. *Sharks.* Garden City, NY: Doubleday, 1987.

Blassingame, Wyatt. *Wonders of Sharks.* New York: Dodd, Mead, 1984.

Brown, Robin. *The Lure of Dolphins.* New York: Avon, 1979.

Bunting, Eve. *The Sea World Book of Sharks.* San Diego, CA: Sea World, 1979.

———. *The Great White Shark.* New York: J. Messner, 1982.

Clark, Eugenie. *Lady with a Spear.* New York: Harpers, 1953.

Coupe, Sheena. *Sharks.* New York: Facts on File, 1990.

Emberlin, Diane. *Contributions of Women—Science.* Minneapolis, MN: Dillon Press, 1977.

Facklam, Margery. *What Does the Crow Know?* San Francisco: Sierra Club Books for Young Readers, 1994.

Freedman, Russell. *Sharks.* New York: Holiday House, 1985.

Gibbons, Gail. *Sharks.* New York: Holiday House, 1992.

Langley, Andrew. *The World of Sharks.* New York: Bookwright Press, 1988.

Lawrence, R. D. *Shark! Nature's Masterpiece.* Shelbury, VT: Chapters, 1994.

MacQuitty, Miranda. *Shark.* New York: Knopf, 1992.

Maestro, Betsy. *A Sea Full of Sharks.* New York: Scholastic, 1990.

Markle, Sandra. *Outside and Inside Sharks.* New York: Atheneum Books for Young Readers, 1996.

McGovern, Ann. *Shark Lady: True Adventures of Eugenie Clark.* New York: Four Winds Press, 1978.

Patent, Dorothy. *How Smart Are Animals?* San Diego, CA: Harcourt Brace Jovanovich, 1990.

Perrine, Doug. *Sharks.* Stillwater, MN: Voyager Press, 1995.

Reed, Don. *Sevengill: The Shark and Me.* New York: Knopf, 1986.

Robson, Denny. *Sharks.* New York: Gloucester Press, 1992.

Romashko, Sandra. *Shark: Lord of the Sea.* Miami, FL: Windward, 1984.

Sattler, Helen. *Fish Facts and Bird Brains.* New York: Lodestar Books, 1984.

Wexo, John. *Sharks.* Mankato, MN: Creative Education, 1989.

Wilson, Lynn. *Sharks!* New York: Platt and Munk, 1992.

Consult your librarian for additional titles.

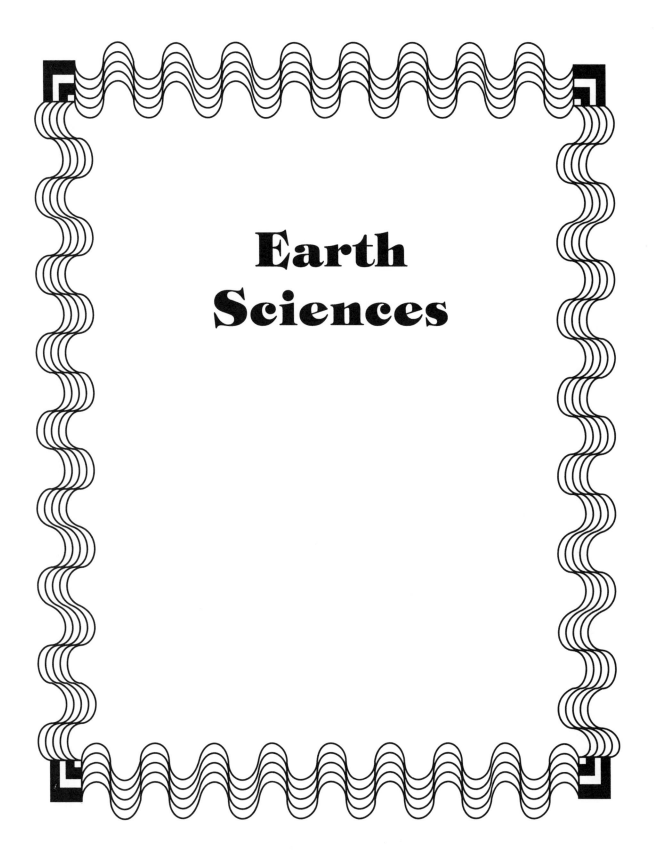

Earth
Sciences

A "Gold Medal" Speck of Light

A Story of Maria Mitchell's Discovery of a New Comet in 1847

➤ **A Point to Ponder**

A pre-story question to focus student attention and interest on the story's central science theme—What is a comet? Is a comet different than a planet? How? What is its "tail" made out of?

➤ **Science Curriculum Links**

This story deals with the earth science field of astronomy. In particular, it focuses on comets and on the process of astronomical observation.

Use this story to introduce a unit on the stars, the night sky, amateur astronomers, or astronomy in general.

➤ **Key Picture-Maker Words**

The following words create mental pictures important to the understanding of this story. However, not all your students may be familiar with each of them. Here are ways to quickly review these words and concepts to ensure that your students get the most out of these moments in science.

1. **Inventory:** An inventory is a list of the items present. Make an inventory of the things in your desk. Make an inventory of the things you are wearing. A library inventory is simply a list of all the books present in the library. Why do you think it's important to make inventories?

2. **Telescope:** A telescope is a tube with special glass lenses to greatly magnify the image seen through the telescope. Where have you seen telescopes? Who uses telescopes?

   Astronomers use powerful telescopes so they can focus on, and study, tiny specks of star light your eye can't even see when you look up into the night sky.

   The opposite of a telescope is a microscope. What does a microscope do? What do you see with a microscope?

3. **Constellation:** A constellation is a group of stars. Combining stars into constellations is a convenient way for people to talk about groups of stars and areas of the night sky.

   The best-known constellation in the Northern Hemisphere is the Big Dipper. Can you find the Big Dipper? In this story Maria Mitchell looked through her telescope at Cassiopeia, another well-known constellation near the North Star. What other constellations, or groups of stars, do you know? Which ones can you find?

4. **Nebulae:** When we look into the night sky we often think that every dot of light we see is a star. This is not true. A good example of something that is not a star is a nebula. A nebula is an immense cloud of gas and dust.

   From many thousands of light-years away, a nebula looks like a point of light, just like a star. But a good telescope will reveal that the colors reflected by nebulae are different than stars, and the look of nebulae is different, even though they still look like fuzzy white dots.

5. **Comet:** A comet is a chunk of rock, surrounded by ice, that races around the Sun in a long orbit. While the Earth makes one revolution around the Sun each year, comets can take 100 or even 1,000 years to make one full lap around their elongated orbits.

   As a comet nears the Sun, part of its ice coating warms and streams off the comet, forming a long, icy tail. In the spring of 1997, comet Hale-Bopp passed very close to Earth. This comet and its tail were clearly visible, even without a telescope or binoculars.

6. **Chronometer:** Chronometer is another word for clock, but a special kind of clock. Chronometers are very accurate clocks used in navigation to determine the position of a ship. During the days of great sailing ships, if a chronometer got off even a little bit, as our modern watches and clocks often do, the captain would miscalculate the position of his ship and the ship would be lost. A chronometer was the most important piece of equipment on a seventeenth-, eighteenth-, or nineteenth-century sailing ship.

A "Gold Medal" Speck of Light

In 1847 you could hear the creak of wooden ships' decks, the clanging of the channel buoys, the smell of salt air, and the screeching of seagulls everywhere on Nantucket Island. Flat, marshy ground surrounded the town of Nantucket on three sides. On the fourth side a busy harbor led out to an endless flat sea. The masts of whaling ships were the tallest points for miles in any direction.

Nantucket Island sat off the southern shore of Massachusetts. With most of the men at sea, Nantucket always looked like a town inhabited only by women, children, and dogs.

Every person in Nantucket learned to tell time by the stars. The lifeblood of the town beat with the ebb and flow of the tides.

But there were *some* things in Nantucket that ran according to the clock instead of the rhythm of the sea. The public library was one of these. It opened at noon each day and closed exactly at 5:00 in the afternoon—except for Saturday, when the library stayed open until 8:00, and Sunday, when it never opened at all.

At five minutes to twelve each day Maria Mitchell, the Nantucket librarian, walked through the front gate of her family's house at the west edge of town and started the short walk downtown to open the library. Maria loved her job at the library. She loved books and had read every book in the library. She thought reading was important and wanted to help decide what the children of Nantucket read. But she especially loved her library job because it let her stay up most nights studying the stars and sleep late each morning.

Studying the stars at night had been part of Maria's life since she was five. One of her father's jobs had been to check the chronometers on whaling ships before they put out to sea. To do that he made a series of very careful measurements during the night through his telescope while his assistant (Maria) recorded and checked the chronometer's time for each event. When she was seven, Maria got to use her father's telescope. Maria got her own telescope when she was eight.

The daily pattern of Maria's life had changed little by the fall of 1847, when she was 29. She still lived at home with her father and three brothers. She worked each day at the library. She studied the stars each evening—*if* it was clear, and *if* the Moon wasn't out to obscure faint stars with its great wash of reflected sunlight.

From *Stepping Stones to Science*. © 1997 Kendall Haven. Teacher Ideas Press. (800) 237-6124.

October 1st, 1847 was a busy day for Maria at the library. The annual inventory of books by the library board of directors would begin tomorrow. In addition to all her normal duties, Maria had to check and straighten the many shelves of books and sneak her stash of secret "lost" books back into the children's area. Anytime Maria saw the children of Nantucket eyeing a book she didn't think they should read, she would conveniently "lose" the book. All these "lost" books had to reappear on the shelves before the director's inventory.

When she closed and locked the library doors at 5:15 that evening, Maria was dead tired. She trudged home toward the setting sun, feeling a brisk hint of coming fall chill in the air. She realized it would be a crystal-clear night. The thought made her weariness melt away. Better yet, the quarter moon was already on its way down toward the western horizon. It would set before midnight. From midnight on, the sky would be perfect for stargazing.

Maria ate dinner with her family and lay down for a short nap, setting her alarm for 11:45. When it went off, she rose, washed the sleep from her face with cold water, and carried her telescope into the backyard. The sky was crisp, clear, and pitch black. The stars seemed to leap out of the heavens at her.

She began her usual slow sweep across the constellations, noting and recording the position and amount of light radiated by each major star. Mars and Jupiter were both plainly visible. Through her telescope she could clearly see the famed canals on Mars, and could even make out some detail on Jupiter's distant surface. Then she turned past the planets to her favorite celestial formations: nebulae. She carefully noted the colors of light radiating from each, and paused to watch and enjoy these wondrous sights.

About 1:30 AM she turned toward the last of the constellations in her normal sweep and began to wonder what she would choose to study in greater depth this sparkling evening. She scanned past Cassiopeia, and. . . .

What was that? A faint white speck where there was supposed to be only black, empty space! She had almost missed it because it wasn't supposed to be there.

Fine-tuning the focus of her telescope, she stared at the distant dot of light. Her heart began to pound. Her breath came more rapidly. This was something new. It hadn't been there two nights ago when she last looked at this quadrant of the sky. What was it?

Maria dashed inside for her father's telescope. His was more powerful than hers—not as good for general sweeps of the sky, but better for detailed study. Excitedly she set up her father's telescope next to her own. Her hands trembled with anticipation, making the telescope wiggle as she rushed to look through it.

It seemed an eternity before she aimed and focused her father's powerful telescope. And there it was! A heavenly body she had never seen before, a faint dust or ice trail scattered out behind it. She could already tell it had moved relative to the stars near it. This was a comet. It could only be a comet.

But there was no record, no listing for this comet. Was it some conveniently "lost" comet snuck back into place before a heavenly inventory? Or could it possibly be a *new* comet? Could she be the first human to gaze at this chunk of rock speeding through space nearer to the Earth? Now her heart truly pounded. Was it possible that a simple librarian in Nantucket, Massachusetts, with barely a high school education, could be the first to discover a new comet?

All astronomers around the world, including Maria, had read that the King of Denmark was offering a gold medal to the first person to discover a new comet. Could this be Maria's gold medal comet?

While she traced her new comet's progress across the sky, 1:30 AM became 5:30. As a dawning day's light hid the stars and her family awoke, Maria rushed in to share her news with her father. Maria was far too excited to sleep, and immediately wrote letters to William Bond at the Harvard Observatory and to Joseph Henry, director of the Smithsonian Institution in Washington, D.C.

However, Nantucket mail only left the island twice a week on the mail boat. Maria's letter did not leave Nantucket until October 4th. On October 3d two other astronomers, one in England, one in Rome, found, and claimed the discovery of, Maria's new comet.

A flurry of letters, claims, and charges sped back and forth for more than a year before the Danish gold medal was officially awarded to Maria in early 1849. But as grand as the trip to Denmark and her shiny medal were, neither could compare with the thrill of that crystal-clear night of October 1, 1847, when Maria Mitchell realized the secret dream of every amateur astronomer: discovering something new in the heavens. With the medal came fame and offers to work as an astronomer and teach at a university. But that is another story.

■   ■   ■

From *Stepping Stones to Science*. © 1997 Kendall Haven. Teacher Ideas Press. (800) 237-6124.

Follow-Up Activities

Maria Mitchell spent many years working to understand the night sky and the many kinds of heavenly bodies that fill it up.

Here are some fun, easy, and powerful activities you can do to better understand how astronomers mark the locations of distant stars and how stars move across the sky over the course of a night or year.

Topics to Talk About

1. Why do all stars in the sky look alike? (*Really, they don't. They are all distant light sources, and so look like points of light. But if you look closely, some look bigger and brighter, while others look dimmer or smaller. Some blink slightly. Some shine off-white, their light being tinged either yellow or red. While these differences may seem small, they are really gigantic differences between different heavenly bodies.*) Do planets and stars look different to the naked eye? (*No. You need a telescope to see the differences. They do, however, move differently across the sky from night to night. This motion can be tracked by the naked eye for planets closest to Earth.*)

2. Do comets look different than planets and stars? (*Yes. Comets have a "tail." This tail is really a trail of ice particles streaming off the comet as it nears the sun. Like planets, comets do not create light, but only reflect the sun's light. They appear dimmer than light-creating stars. Finally, comets move across the sky in different patterns than stars and planets. Even if their tails are invisible, their motion marks them as comets.*)

Activities to Do

1. Necessary Equipment:

   • One large (at least 6") plastic compass—the semicircular 180° style

   • One plastic or wooden 12" ruler

   • One small weight (at least four oz.). Metal washers, a heavy eraser, or even a large bolt will do.

   • Several feet of string, yarn, or thick white thread

   • A magnetic compass

   • One wooden stake and two six-foot lengths of thick string or light rope

   • Copies of "Student Worksheet," page 149

2. Your Own Sextant to the Stars.

Astronomers now use computers, telescopes, and satellites to locate our position relative to the stars and to track the movement of the stars. However, for centuries before these things were invented, humans used sextants, and before that quadrants, to chart the position of the stars. Even a simple, homemade "sextant" is a powerful tool for following the movement and cycles of the night skies.

Two measurements are needed to mark where a star is in the sky. Both measurements are recorded as angles—one up from horizontal, the other measured around from north. The first of these is called an *elevation angle*, or how high up in the sky the star is. The second is called *azimuth*, or the direction to the star, measured on a compass.

It is easy to build your own sextant and compare its accuracy with those of your classmates.

- Gather ruler, compass, string, weight, and tape. Tape your ruler onto the compass so that the ruled edge runs from the compass's origin point (center) through one "zero degree" mark and extends beyond. See the diagram on the enclosed worksheet.

- Next, thread your string through the compass's origin hole and knot its upper end. Tape or tie the string's lower end to your weight. This line will fall straight toward Earth.

- Hold the compass with curved edge down, and you have a simple, homemade sextant. Sight along the ruler's edge at a distant star. Have someone else read the angle (in degrees) at the curved bottom of the compass where your string crosses the plastic arc of your compass. This is the elevation angle to the star you are marking.

An elevation angle tells us how high in the sky a star is. An elevation angle of 90 percent means the star is straight overhead. An elevation angle of 0 percent means the star sits on the level horizon. An elevation angle of 45 percent means the star is halfway up the sky.

However, the angle you read on your homemade sextant is not the elevation angle to your star, because you are holding the compass upside down. You must subtract this angle from 90 degrees to get the elevation angle to the star you measured.

Elevation angle is one of the two measures you need to locate a star. The other measure is the direction, or azimuth, to the star.

There are two simple ways of measuring azimuth. Try both and see which gives you better results. The first way is to use a magnetic compass. It is easy, but as you will see, a little awkward.

- Align the magnetic compass so that the compass's floating arrow points along the north line on the compass's dial. Now hold your sextant over the compass and sight along the ruler to your chosen star. As you fix your eye on the distant star, have a helper watch the compass and sextant to ensure that the compass stays lined up with north and that you hold your sextant directly over the middle of the compass.

From *Stepping Stones to Science.* © 1997 Kendall Haven. Teacher Ideas Press. (800) 237-6124.

- When the magnetic compass and sextant are correctly aimed and aligned, glance down and read the degree (angle) over which your sextant is resting. This is the azimuth to your star.

- Your readings will be in this example form: azimuth—223 degrees, elevation—41 degrees. These readings define a point about halfway up in the southwestern sky.

- The second way to measure azimuth requires one stake (pointed stick), two six-foot segments of thick white string, and two rocks.

- Pound the stake partway into the ground at the spot where you plan to stand for your measurements. Next find the North Star. (Use the Big Dipper as a guide to locating the North Star or ask an adult for help if you are not sure which star is the North Star.) Stand with both heels touching the stake and sight toward the North Star. Have a helper stretch the first of your strings along this line from your stake toward the North Star.

- This string points due north. Place a heavy rock on the end of this string to hold it in place.

- Now sight from your stake toward some distant star. Have your helper stretch out the second string from the stake in line with your sighting toward this new star. Have your helper secure this line with a second rock.

- Use your semicircular compass to measure the angle between these two strings. Is this angle the azimuth toward your chosen star? Maybe.

- Remember, azimuth is measured in a clockwise circle of 360 degrees around from north (0°), through east (90°), south (180°), and west (270°) before returning to north (360° or 0°). Your compass can only measure 180 degrees. If you measured your string angle clockwise from north, the angle you measured is the azimuth to this star. If, however, you measured counter-clockwise from north to the string pointing at your star, you must subtract the angle you measured from 360 degrees to find the correct azimuth.

- As a check on everyone's homemade sextants, have all students measure the elevation and azimuth to the same star *at the same time* on the same evening. Try both methods described above to calculate the azimuth. Write the elevation angle and azimuth you record on the worksheet.

- Compare readings during class the next day. Did everyone measure approximately the same elevation and azimuth? There was probably quite a difference between the measurements from some of your classmates. What happened? Did the star move that quickly? No, it didn't. The answer is that it is very hard to make these measurements with homemade equipment. Errors creep into the measurement process. The more you use your homemade sextant—the more you try to measure the position of the stars— the better you will become at it.

- Does your simple homemade sextant give you a feeling for how ships at sea are able to calculate their position by measuring the angle from their ship to known stars? Can you see the advantage of knowing the stars and their positions if you were lost?

# STUDENT WORKSHEET
for Activities to Do
following a story about **Maria Mitchell**

1. Building Your Own Sextant.

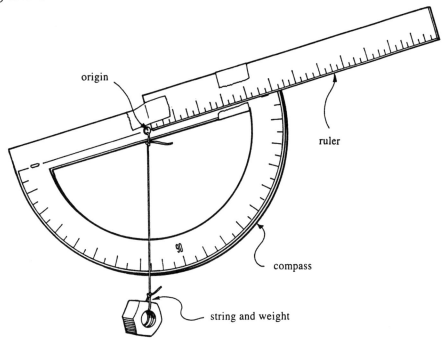

2. My measurement of a star.

The star we chose to measure is: _____

1. Elevation Angle.

   The angle I read = _____

   90° - this angle = my elevation angle = _____

2. Azimuth.

   The azimuth I read on a compass = _____

   The azimuth I read using ropes = _____

   (If I read counter-clockwise from North to get this
   angle, I had to subtract the angle from 360° to get my
   azimuth instead of using the angle I read.)

Additional Reading

Good references in the children's library for further reading on astronomy, comets, and Maria Mitchell's experiments include:

Asimov, Isaac. *Asimov on Astronomy.* Garden City, NY: Doubleday Books, 1975.

Baker, Rachel. *America's First Woman Astronomer: Maria Mitchell.* New York: J. Messner, 1980.

Berry, Erich. *Stars in My Pocket.* New York: Day, 1980.

Degani, Meir. *Astronomy Made Simple.* New York: Doubleday, 1976.

Ferris, Jeri. *What Are You Figuring Now?* Minneapolis, MN: Carolrhoda Books, 1988.

Fichter, George. *Comets and Meteors.* New York: F. Watts, 1982.

Fisher, David. *The Origin and Evolution of Our Particular Universe.* New York: Atheneum, 1988.

Fradin, Dennis. *Comets, Asteroids, and Meteors.* Chicago: Childrens Press, 1984.

Harwit, Martin. *Cosmic Discovery.* Cambridge, MA: MIT Press, 1984.

Hoyle, Fred. *Highlights in Astronomy.* New York: Freeman, 1975.

McPherson, Stephanie. *Rooftop Astronomer.* Minneapolis, MN: Carolrhoda Books, 1990.

Melen, Grace. *Maria Mitchell.* New York: Bobbs-Merrill, 1974.

Milton, Jacqueline. *Astronomy: An Introduction for the Amateur Astronomer.* Boston: Scribner's, 1978.

Moore, Patrick. *Comets.* Boston: Scribner's, 1986.

———. *The Amateur Astronomer.* New York: W. W. Norton, 1990.

Oles, Carole. *Night Watches: Inventions on the Life of Maria Mitchell.* Cambridge, MA: Alice James Books, 1985.

Overbye, Dennis. *Lonely Hearts of the Cosmos.* New York: HarperCollins, 1991.

Ridpath, Ian. *The Young Astronomer's Handbook.* New York: Arco Publishing, 1984.

Ronan, Colin. *Man Probes the Universe.* New York: Natural History Project, 1974.

———. *The Natural History of the Universe.* New York: Macmillan, 1991.

Serafini, Anthony. *Legends in Their Own Time.* New York: Plenum Press, 1993.

Wayne, Bennett. *Women Who Dared to Be Different.* Champaign, IL: Garrard, 1973.

Wilkie, Katherine. *Maria Mitchell, Star Gazer.* New York: Garrard, 1976.

Consult your librarian for additional titles.

Index

About the Author

A former research scientist, Kendall Haven is the only West Point graduate to ever become a professional storyteller. He holds a Master's Degree in Oceanography and spent six years with the Department of Energy before finding his true passion for storytelling and a very different kind of "truth." He has now performed for close to 3 million people in 40 states, and has won awards for his story-writing and storytelling. He has conducted workshops in over 20 states on storytelling's practical, in-class teaching power, and has become one of the nation's leading advocates for the educational value of storytelling.

Kendall has recorded five audio tapes and published six books of original stories. He has also used his writing talent to create stories for many non-profit organizations, including The American Cancer Society and the Institute for Mental Health Initiatives. He recently created a national award-winning adventure drama for National Public Radio on the effects of watching television. His first Teacher Ideas Press book of 50 science stories, *Marvels of Science*, makes the history and process of science fascinating and compelling. *Amazing American Women* illuminates 40 fascinating and little known women's stories in American history. His third book, *Great Moments in Science*, was released in early 1996. Three additional titles are in development and will be released in 1997.

Haven's most recent awards include the 1995 and 1996 Storytelling World Silver Award for best Story Anthology, the 1993 International Festival Association Silver Award for best Education Program, the 1992 Corporation for Public Broadcasting Silver Award for best Children's Public Radio Production, and the 1991 Award for Excellence in California Education. He has twice been an American Library Association "Notable Recording Artist," and is the only storyteller in the United States with three entries in the ALA's *Best of the Best for Children*.

Haven is founder and Chair of the International Whole Language Umbrella Storytelling Interest Group, and is on the Board of Directors as well as the Educational Advisory Committee of the National Storytelling Association. He is a co-director of the Sonoma Storytelling Festival, past four-year Chair of the Bay Area Storytelling Festival, and founder of storytelling festivals in Las Vegas, NV; Boise, ID; and Mariposa, CA.

He lives with his wife in the rolling Sonoma County grape vineyards in rural Northern California.